YOUR KEYS
OUR HOME

Debbie & Michael Campbell
THE SENIOR NOMADS'
Incredible Airbnb Journey

Credits:
Designed by: Debbie Campbell, Emily Perrone
Production Design: Toby Cowan, Performance Design Group
Edited by: Luana Cowan, Carol Franco and Kent Lineback

Photos: When we started our journey we took happy snaps just like
anyone else – mostly to be shared with family and friends and
on our personal blog. We never imagined we would write a book and
wish we had dozens of "award-winning photos" to help tell our story.
All the photos in this book were taken with our trusty iPhone 5s
by one of us, or if we wanted a photo of the two us we asked
one of those kind strangers we mention in the dedication.

———————————————

ISBN 978-1-5390-1464-5

Printed in U.S.A.

This book is dedicated to
the countless people
who helped us along the way,
affirming the kindness
of strangers everywhere.

Acknowledgements

If writing a book can be considered a journey, we would like to acknowledge the many people who helped us along the way to this final destination. Some were strangers who have become friends. Others were professionals who gave us sage advice and also became friends.

First on our list is Chip Conley, the exuberant Head of Hospitality and Global Strategy at Airbnb. Chip was captivated by our Senior Nomads' story right from the start. When we told him we wanted to write this book, he was immediately on board and became our biggest supporter.

Next come our editors and collaborators, literary agent Carol Franco and her husband Kent Lineback, a professional writer and writing coach. They found us after the New York Times ran a story about our travels in February 2015 and were the first to suggest we write a book. We had never written a book, never thought about writing a book, and certainly never believed we'd ever hold a book in our hands with our names on it. Without their expert guidance, it would not have been possible.

You actually can judge a book by its cover and that is why we chose Emily Perrone, one of the finest graphic designers we know, to create ours. Emily worked for Debbie for ten years at Tip Top Creative and it was a pleasure to work with her again.

Turning to the first page and every page thereafter, we thank Toby Cowan for his heroic efforts to not only produce a beautiful book, but keep us on track and manage the entire project while we continued to travel. Thankfully Toby's wife, Luana, is a professional proofreader who has no patience for miscreant commas or creative spelling.

Well before we had the confidence to start telling our story, we had a great coach in Billy Meyer who helped us fine-tune our presentation at the 2015 Airbnb Open. He convinced us that we could, in fact, inspire others to follow their dream. Billy introduced us to Dan Zadra, a well-known writer of inspirational books, who also helped set us on the path to telling our story.

And, of course, we embrace our family – all four of our children: Alistair, Kelly, Mary and Christopher, along with their spouses and a fine collection of grandchildren. They never wavered in their support as we sold our possessions and traveled wherever the wind took us, even though it meant long stretches of being apart. We could not have done it otherwise.

Lastly, this journey would have been nothing more than a few Excel spreadsheets and a tattered wish list without Airbnb's vision that we can belong anywhere, and with hosts who bring that vision to life. In every city, in every country, and in every Airbnb, we were welcomed by hosts who made our experience in their homes memories we will always treasure.

Contents

Foreword

In early 2015, I read a lengthy article about Michael and Debbie Campbell in *The New York Times*. I was charmed and, admittedly, intrigued by this couple who've been together nearly forty years. They said they "had one more adventure in them" before retirement so they set off on a world tour staying only in Airbnb homes.

Part of my intrigue was professional, part personal. Could we have them speak at our Airbnb Open in November 2015? And, could I live that same sojourning lifestyle in a few years when I hit retirement age? I also felt a kinship with them because I learned of Airbnb, as a long-time boutique hotelier, at almost exactly the same time as they did, near the end of 2012. Within months, without knowing each other, we put our trust in Airbnb – the Campbells as globetrotters and me in my new unexpected role as head of hospitality for the company.

Over the course of last year, my charm turned into admiration as I helped prep the Campbells for their stage time at the

Airbnb Open in Paris. They helped me to see hospitality is truly just another word for humanity. While I've said to our host community, "Airbnb can make you both a better host and a better human," I realized that this equation for hospitality and humanity needed to include the guest side as well. As Debbie says, "as guests we've learned the universal language of courtesy." Needless to say, Michael and Debbie were one of Airbnb Open's most appreciated speakers last year, so we brainstormed about what we could cook up for this year.

You're holding the result of that brainstorm in your hands. The Campbells have so much to share, we believed it was time for them to write a book especially for our attendees of the Airbnb Open in Los Angeles. Given their beautiful stories and helpful wisdom, this book is perfectly suited to wanderlusting Airbnb guests, couples imagining how they can travel better together, and those in the second half of their lives wondering what's next.

But, the book is really written for you, our passionate and engaged hosts who want to learn more about how to surprise and delight your guests. Of course, once you've read this book, you'll wish that all your guests were as thoughtful and interesting as Michael and Debbie. But, don't just read this for entertainment value. Pull out a highlighter or a pen because I bet you'll write a lot of notes in the margins as you read their practical tips on how to please both the novice and veteran Airbnb guest.

When the number of countries you've traveled on your never-ending adventure starts to rival your age, you're either very young or very hearty. As you'll find in this book, their travels have helped to keep them young now that they've been on the road for more than three years with Airbnb experiences in fifty countries. A wise yogi once wrote, "Travel light, live light, spread the light, be the light." No words better describe the Campbells' role as Airbnb's most inspiring and luminescent guests in the world.

Chip Conley
Head of Global Hospitality and Strategy at Airbnb

"...Michael and Debbie are not tourists, they are two great travelers, like those of past centuries moved by their thirst for knowledge. They don't simply pass by, they stop to observe the new landscapes, to understand the people of the places where they are. They are not in a hurry, they know that the pleasure is in the heart of the stones of the cities and its people. They do not seek the comfort of big hotels that keep them away from real life, they want to be one of the people who live in the cities where they stop. They seek knowledge to magnify their young hearts. Thank you for choosing my house in your long journey."

— Host, Enrique A. / Madrid, Spain
December 2014

Introduction
Home on the road

Our Senior Nomads' story began when we started pondering what might be next for us as retirement approached. Would we keep working? Move to another city? Join the Peace Corps? Debbie kept insisting, "I think we have one more adventure in us." And we did.

The seed for this adventure was planted at Christmastime in 2012. Our middle daughter Mary, her French husband Gregoire, and our toddling granddaughter Colette were visiting from Paris. One night over dinner, Mary asked a seemingly innocent question, "Have you heard of Airbnb?" We had not.

That's when she unveiled her plan. She had been perusing the bulletin board in our kitchen and found a dream list of countries we wanted to visit. "Why not stop working right now and travel full time using Airbnb — starting in Paris of course! I'll show you how it works."

The idea was intriguing. We weren't strangers to travel. Michael raced Formula 3 cars throughout Europe when he was in his early twenties. Years later, as a family, we lived in London and traveled often with our four young children. Even when we returned to Seattle, five years later, we continued to travel together. And now all four of our adult children are intrepid travelers on their own.

Over the next few days we asked ourselves if maybe, just maybe, Mary had come up with an idea that was perfect for us at that time in our lives. We crunched the numbers, did the research, and decided we'd give it a try.

In the summer of 2013 we set out and have been traveling non-stop ever since, happily living our lives exclusively in Airbnb homes. In that time, we've visited 152 cities in 50 countries and stayed in 110 different homes.

It is now the summer of 2016 and, as we write this, we are still on the road — and we are having the time of our lives. We've learned more about the world, past and present, than any university could have taught us (even though they tried) and made hundreds of friends along the way. Best of all, we've found that doing with far less lets us experience so much more.

We recently sold our house in Seattle. So now, without a home of our own, we truly consider your homes our home! We hope this book will make you laugh, bring back memories of guests – good and bad – and most of all remind you that what you do as hosts does more than make our stay memorable. You're changing the world for travelers like us, one night at a time.

Thank you for what you do. Keep hosting. Keep welcoming strangers into your homes. And keep giving us your keys – keys that allow us to belong anywhere.

Debbie and Michael Campbell
The Senior Nomads

1

House Hunting
How we choose our Airbnbs

"I haven't been everywhere but it's on my list."

– Susan Sontag

Even before we set out on our Senior Nomads' journey, we'd seek out real estate offices whenever we were in a new city. We'd press our noses up against the window to pour over the enticing photos and descriptions. Then we'd ask ourselves: What would it be like to live there? What would it cost? If we could pick just one house, which would it be? That's the same flight of imagination we take every time we land on Airbnb's website.

Now we house hunt on Airbnb.

For several years Michael and I had been contemplating retirement scenarios, everything from a cabin on a lake or a smaller home in Seattle to becoming ESL teachers or Woofing (picking olives in Italy, for example). None of them included a wanderlust lifestyle, and at the time we hadn't even heard of Airbnb. But once our daughter Mary showed us the website, it seemed possible that we could create an affordable lifestyle that allowed us to explore the world, living in one new house after another. We were hooked.

We sold our cars and our sailboat, leased our house and sold or gave away most everything in it, and rented a small storage unit for the few things we couldn't bear to part with. We bought two large REI rolling suitcases and a couple of daypacks to contain the essentials we'd need on the road – including bed pillows. In July of 2013 we waved goodbye to friends and family in Seattle and headed to Europe for a six-month trial run.

It was hard to say goodbye.

We eased into our new lifestyle in Paris to be near Mary and Gregoire and our youngest grandchildren. We were able to stay for free in a friend's apartment in Montmartre just two blocks away from their place. Two weeks later we all piled onto a train bound for Quiberon, a seaside village in Brittany where

Gregoire's family lives, to indulge in the French tradition of *les grandes vacances* for most of August. This time we stayed in an apartment over Gregoire's grandmother's garage, also for free. Things were going well!

A family reunion in Paris.

But before we headed to the beach, the time had come when we needed to make our first real Airbnb booking. As we sat with Mary and Gregoire at the kitchen table and opened the website, the first mild case of panic swept over us. At that moment we fully grasped that the success of our venture hinged on finding homes within our budget. What if the budget we created wasn't realistic? What if we couldn't find anything we liked? What if there were no listings in the city of our choice?

When the site asked "Where to?" we typed "Amsterdam,

Netherlands" and the dates for our first two-week stay. That's when the second wave of panic struck with the opposite problem – we were overwhelmed with choices! Over 1,000 listings flooded the search results.

All we needed was one – but how could we find the right one? It was time to put our fledgling Airbnb skills to the test. We checked a few more filter boxes such as "entire house" and "wireless Internet" and gingerly pressed the search button again. We still had more than 500 listings to choose from. Now what? In a classic case of "we didn't know then what we know now" we started wading through the choices. Eventually, we understood we could reduce the deluge by adding more filters, such as "one bedroom." We also figured out the pricing scale and zoomed the map to the center of the city where we prefer to stay. That reduced the selection considerably.

Still, we were dazzled by the images, especially the listings with enticing hero shots. It was the real estate listings in the window fantasy experience times 100. Which one should we "buy"? Our favorite Amsterdam listing showed two Dutch bikes with jaunty baskets that came with the house. We pictured ourselves sitting high on the saddles blending smoothly into the streams of friendly cyclists with a little "brrring brrring" of our bells – just like the locals. We were getting excited.

Our very first Airbnb.

Finally, after a lot of back and forth and Michael's tenacity, we had a dozen picks safely in our Wish List (once we figured out what a Wish List was). Now it was time to make that first inquiry to the hosts.

In our two-person team, Michael is Chief Travel Planner, or CTP, thanks to his long and successful career as a sports and events promoter. He relishes researching, planning, budgeting, plotting a course, and closing a deal – all the skills needed to make this life "event" a success. My own skills shine as a writer, graphic designer, creative spirit, and cook. My role is Head Provisioner and Entertainment Director. We're a great match.

In this first Airbnb foray, Michael took charge of the communication and negotiations with our potential hosts. However, even this sage marketing master wasn't sure how to approach it. What to say? How much to say? Would having no history as

guests be a problem? He was also concerned about our ages –
at the time 57 and 67. Maybe hosts wouldn't want to rent to
"old" people – what if one of us keeled over in their living room?
Finally, he wasn't certain about pricing and how it worked. He
understood that individual hosts set the price for their listings
so it would seem a guest could negotiate a bit. But how much
of a discount could we request without appearing cheap? He
also planned to confirm the dates we requested in case the
host's calendar hadn't been updated.

Michael began by contacting our top three choices. He
wasn't sure what would happen if we reached out to a dozen
hosts and received a dozen offers – or how we would cope if
nobody would have us. His email consisted of a handful of crisp
sentences expressing our interest and asking for a slightly low-
er rate. He didn't go into much detail except to say we were
a couple in our 50s/60s, nor did he mention our plan to live
exclusively in Airbnbs. At that time, we didn't understand the
importance of profiles and reviews.

Once the inquiries were sent, we held our breath and hoped
we'd done it correctly. Happily we heard back from all three
hosts within a few hours with two friendly, positive responses and
one where the dates were no longer available. Michael finished
the booking process for our first choice and we both eased the
tension from our shoulders and felt great about having our first
Airbnb locked in.

Our host, Rutger, was happy to offer a small discount and was patient with our questions. Unfortunately, he would not be in town during our stay but gave us great directions to his place and assured us his good friend and next-door neighbor Maria would meet us with a warm welcome. Not only did she meet us, but when I asked if there was a toaster she said "not yet!" and hustled off to the nearest kitchen store and returned with a deluxe model an hour later. We were impressed. Rutger also offered the use of those beautiful Dutch bikes we fell in love with, and we did use them — just not with the same chutzpah we'd imagined.

Since that first search, more than 120 Airbnbs ago, we have become experts at choosing our next home. And, the truth is, house hunting is now the most enjoyable part of our travel planning as we combine our skills and personalities to find our next front door. Usually we sit at a big table and peer into our computer screens researching a destination and then searching Airbnb. (Another early "aha" moment was discovering we could both be in our Airbnb account at the same time!) Now we each pop our favorites into the Wish List to review together later.

If there is tension around our process it comes from not being consistent. Just like real house hunting, we can be prone to budget creep (exceeding our ideal spending threshold); one of us will push to spend more because a place is just too great to pass up, rationalizing we'll spend less in a more affordable city down the road. Other times one of us will toss in listings based on a quick glance at the pictures without considering the other agreed-upon criteria like entire home, WiFi, proximity to public transportation and, of course, reviews. When it comes time to go over the Wish List together, tempers can flare if we have to remove half the listings because one of us wasn't following protocol. Part of the fun, though, is defending favorites that do pass the test and see whose choice prevails. Of course, that creates apprehension knowing whatever lies behind the front door was *your* absolute, I'm-not-budging pick.

When we start a new search, the photos are the main draw because they provide a window into our soon-to-be home. The pictures that feature a warm, inviting space get our attention. We skip over ones with nothing but a few sticks of IKEA furniture and no personality. Our goal is to find a place that shows the host cares more about their guests' experience than the income from a spare (and sparse) apartment.

Once we've found several favorites, we scrutinize the details in every photo and try not to fall deeply in love with a listing based on eye candy alone. We examine the bedroom shots for reading lights and closet space. We cook most of our meals at home so we scour the kitchen for clues on what might be available for cooking – is that a toaster on the counter? Excellent! Once I spotted a shiny red Kitchenaid mixer and literally swooned! We look for natural light and hopefully a little access to outdoor space, and a large table where we can spread out. We skip over close-ups of ceramic frogs and unfocused shots of lavender bundles, but we do like to see things that express a host's personality. We don't dwell on more than one beauty shot of the toilet. We are wary of towels folded into swans because, well, normal people just don't do that. And we take it as a bad sign if there are more pictures of nearby attractions than the inside of the apartment – although we love seeing the view from our potential windows or balcony.

You'll find me in the kitchen.

The number of reviews a listing contains has risen to the top of our checklist – the more the better. We read them carefully to confirm what was described in the listing. If the host wasn't responsive, the bed sagged in the middle, the next door neighbor's son was a fledgling garage-band drummer, or those "nearby attractions" in the photos were ten miles away, a previous guest will have noted it. On the other hand, if the host was over-the-top warm and welcoming, the listing was "better than the pictures," the place was clean, and everything "just outside our front door" really was – we'll see that, too. We also read the host profiles to learn more about why they became hosts and how engaged they are with the Airbnb philosophy. And, of course, now that we know potential hosts can read reviews of us as well, we strive to be 5-star guests. Here is our first ever review:

Michael and Debbie were great guests and one of the reasons you would start renting your place on Airbnb. They where friendly, respectful and clean and according to their blog loved every minute of their stay in Amsterdam. Michael and Debbie you are more than welcome to stay another time!

Rutger
Van Der
Kamp

September 2013

After our first six-month trial run, we returned home for Christmas. But before you could say "Happy New Year!" we were off again, this time unsure when we'd return. It's now been more than three incredible years since we closed the lock on the storage unit – and we've nearly exhausted Europe. We've also explored Russia, Turkey, Israel, Cuba, and Mexico. Who knows where we'll head next? Michael and I still get a thrill when we peer into that Airbnb window on the world and fill in the "Where To?" box. And we continue to be amazed by the

11

sheer number and quality of Airbnb listings we find almost anywhere our imagination takes us. In 55 countries there hasn't been a single time we couldn't find a delightful place to call home.

2

Dear Host

Let's start a conversation

"I met a lot of people in Europe.
I even encountered myself."

– James Baldwin

On that sunny afternoon in Paris when Michael pressed "send" on the emails to our first three potential Airbnb hosts, we really did wonder why anyone would be willing to open their private homes to complete strangers. And why us? Even though we were still a little baffled by the concept, we were counting on it to work. In fact, our entire Senior Nomads' strategy was built around it.

A warm welcome from Yishai in Jerusalem.

Since that first booking we've learned a great deal about communicating with potential hosts, and the engaging back-and-forth between the request and the final booking is as important to our decision on what listing we choose as captivating photos and great reviews.

Here's our look back at our very first email to a host:

> We are interested in staying in your apartment. Are you willing to do the $98 price for these two weeks? We are a married couple in our 50s/60s and currently are in Paris visiting our adult daughter and her family. Please let us know.
>
> Michael, July 2013

After that short, impersonal first inquiry we began to understand it was better to share more information about ourselves and our travels in order to get a conversation going. Below is a more personal email we sent about a year later to a potential host in Sarajevo, Bosnia & Herzegovina:

> Emir - We are an American couple in our 50s and 60s from Seattle traveling in Europe for a year. After quitting our jobs and downsizing, we flew to Europe last July spending the early weeks in France with one of our adult daughters and her family. After that, we moved on to Amsterdam, Copenhagen, Stockholm, Berlin, Milan, Athens, Lisbon and Paris. We spent the holidays in America but came back to Europe last month and have spent time in France and Spain. We are headed to Rome next and on to Istanbul before coming to Sarajevo for a few days next month. Before we make our decision on where to stay, can you confirm that your place is available on these dates? Thank you for your help in advance. We look forward to hearing from you.
>
> Michael, March 2014

We were getting the hang of it. Here is a recent inquiry to a host in Galway, Ireland. It's an example of the way we now communicate with hosts. Just like our travels, our emails have expanded over time!

Dear Irene - Almost three years ago, my wife Debbie and I decided to stop working, downsize, and sell our house in Seattle to travel full time. We have been on the road ever since living in Airbnbs. We have visited 48 countries and stayed in 102 different Airbnb apartments. We are currently in Split, Croatia.

We are both healthy and having the time of our lives. Until something changes, we are planning on continuing our travels. We've actually sold our home in Seattle so we are on the road for the foreseeable future. We call ourselves the Senior Nomads.

Next month we are coming back to Ireland for a second time. Two years ago we visited Dublin and Wexford. On this visit we would like to visit Western Ireland. Your unique apartment over the river looks fantastic and very comfortable and we've read your very complimentary reviews.

1. Is your place available on these dates?

2. What is the best price you can offer?

Because we live year-round in Airbnb homes, we really have to watch what we spend every night. Our budget is $90/night which is below your quoted price. In this instance, we were wondering if you might be willing to make us a Special Offer.

If you would like to learn more about us, we were featured last month in Condé Nast Traveler magazine. You can find the article if you search for "Condé Nast Traveler Senior Nomads".

Please feel free to check out our reviews from previous hosts. Thanks for your help in advance. We look forward to hearing from you and hopefully staying with you next month.

Michael, May 2016

In between these examples fall hundreds of inquiries sent to hosts all over the world. Over time they evolved from that first impersonal communication to more detailed inquiries with information about us and our travels, and even personalized inquiries containing information we gleaned from the Airbnb site about the host's home, profile, and reviews. At times, we even include recent press coverage to help tell our story.

We continue to request a discount, or "Special Offer," especially for a Wish-List favorite that might be slightly over budget. And we still double-check the dates. Then we wait. Of course we hope to hear back immediately from our favorites with enticing responses.

Here are a couple of responses that we loved. The first is from Blanca, our host in Granada, Spain, and the second from Stefanos, our host in Rhodes, Greece.

Clearly, a warm response translates in any language:

Dear Michael, Debbie, Thank you so much for interest in my place, this is perfect place to rest and enjoy the amazing views and the atmosphere of the Albayzin quarter, the old moorish quarter, the location is very good, only a few min walking from the main attractions, bars and restaurants área, but, at same time, its located on a pedestry square, far from cars traffic, where you can hear the birds in the morning and enjoy of a peaceful atmosphere. The flat is very comfortable and warm, it has free wifi and its full equipped, the views from the balcony are so beautifully and i,ll happy to welcome you and show you my places. I'm at your disposal for any question and looking forward to hear from you!

Saludos, Blanca
Granada, Spain November 2014

Dear Mr. Michael that's like a dream to me and I wish I can do the same one day...it is up to Mrs Merkel :) The house is available and I am sure it would be one of the best you stayed during your past holidays. It is less than 5 minutes walk from the center of old town and 10-15 minutes walk to new towns center. Please do not hesitate to contact me as I am here for anything more you might need for having memorable holidays, I will be at your service.

Best Regards Stefanos
Rhodes, Greece March 2015

Happy hosts Stefanos and Gavriela.

Booking Airbnbs with our Cuban hosts pushed remote-host communication to the extreme. Because of the lack of Internet availability for most Cubans, we found we were booking Airbnbs through our potential host's friends or relatives who lived abroad. They in turn would contact the host by phone, relay the booking details, check the calendar, and then get back to us. Until we actually arrived at each front door, we weren't sure if everything had come together. Because Airbnb was already blazing a trail in Cuba, we didn't hesitate to book our rentals because we knew that if anything went wrong they would take care of us. It all worked out, and we thoroughly enjoyed living in five of Cuba's most intriguing cities – and spending time with some of the warmest, most welcoming hosts we've ever met.

Our favorite response came from a Canadian working on behalf of Kiwi, our actual host in La Boca near Trinidad:

Hola Michael, Thanks for your interest and reservation. Kiwi and her adorable family would love to have you stay in their home and will take good care of you. A friendly reminder that no ATM or bank will accept "any" US issued bank cards or credit cards, no matter what your bank is telling you, it will NOT work in CUBA!!! So please make sure to bring all you need to spend with you, or you will get stuck guaranteed! Another thing, in Cuba the exchange rates for American $ is subject to a 10% levy charge on top of the very bad rates they offer Americans... So for example right now the exchange rate is about $0.95cuc for every US $ + a 10% fee on top of that (only applies to US $)... But if you exchange your US cash back home to euros or Canadian $, then exchange that in Cuba, you will be at least 5 to 7% ahead...

Things you will need to bring with you: - Bug spray - All your toiletries (don't expect to buy anything here, its a complete hit and miss, so come prepared with all you will need) - Ear plugs for sleeping!! There are roosters everywhere in Cuba and when one starts they all start, and they go off at the weirdest times, middle of the night and very early mornings!! - Good closed water/beach sandals! There are sharp plants and rocks everywhere.

You can buy travel insurance in the Havana airport, its excellent... your own insurance will only work if you can pay all medical bills upfront and claim back when you have returned and with no access to ATM, its a big risk for American travelers!!! If you need more information the best place to find most accurate info are on the tripadvisor Cuba forums.

If you need help getting to Kiwi's home, please make sure to give her a call asap when you arrive in Cuba so she can help you arrange transportations. The complete address and contact info will be in your reservation page, please make sure to print it and carry with you, also the pictures of the home from street to recognize it easier. Enjoy your trip.

Cheers, Yash
Trinidad via Montreal January 2016

Cuba was a great ride.

Once we've heard back from the hosts we've contacted, usually about a half a dozen or so, we review our choices based on the responses. The more personal and welcoming the response, the more likely we'll book that rental even if a different property offers more of what we're looking for. A truly engaged host who's focused on a great guest experience makes up for a less-than-perfect listing every time.

When we began our journey, we avoided listings with no reviews. Now, with experience, we're willing to be the first guests if a property fits our criteria and the host's response is truly special. Besides, unlike booking a once-in-a-lifetime dream home, we know if a place falls short of our expectations, we have another potentially fabulous home booked down the road.

In April 2015 we reserved an entire house in Haarlem, Netherlands, for a week where we would be the host's first guests. We needed an affordable home large enough for us plus our daughter and her husband who live in Paris with their three young children. Not the easiest criteria to meet, so we had to dig deeper than usual to find the right listing. We found the perfect house with photos of a big kitchen, lots of toys, a fenced yard, and the promise of a family-friendly neighborhood. The host family had small children of their own and decided that listing their home on Airbnb might enable them to travel as a family when their home was rented. Perfect for both parties! We had a delightful exchange about logistics and what to do while we were there. We were able to meet the host family just as they were packing up to head out, and the Dutch kids showed the French kids where to find the toys. Our host Sanne's suggestions on how to spend the national King's Day holiday added to the fun:

> ...That is our holiday when we Celebrate the birthday of our King Willem Alexander. On that day you can go to Amsterdam, together with 2 million other Dutch people, but I really would not advise that. Way too crowded, especially with the kids.
>
> What we always do, we go to a very lovely flea market, 10 minutes walk from our house, in a beautiful neighborhood, where there is a special flea market just for kids. It starts early in the morning, around 09 hrs. All the kids from the neighborhoods are selling their own toys, books, candy and cakes for minimal prices. Very nice atmosphere and for you a way to taste the really Dutch tradition of selling your old stuff on Kings-day. There are concerts and performers all day, too.
>
> The dress for everyone is 'Oranjeplein'. Oranje means orange and orange is our national colour. We have some orange dressing up clothes for children ....
>
> Best regards, Sanne
> Haarlem, Netherlands April 2015

In 2016 we returned to Croatia, one of our favorite countries, to explore it further. We had especially enjoyed our time in Split two years earlier so we started there. On our first pass through the listings available for our dates and price range, we were surprised to see fewer listings than we expected. When we reviewed them again, we noticed one we'd overlooked. It was lovely, and had everything we were looking for – except reviews. We reached out to Jelena, the host, who responded with a lengthy description of her home and surroundings and why it would appeal to us. She also made so many offers to help us during our stay that we just couldn't refuse.

Dear Michael,

First of all thank you for considering our apartment for your stay in Split.

As we started renting our apartment only recently, we do not have any reviews yet, but our first guests will leave in a couple of days, so hopefully there will be a reviews soon.

I am happy to answer your questions so you can much easier decide whether our apartment suits your needs or not. The apartment is available during the requested period and we would very much like to be your hosts and possibly hear some great stories about the travels you did. By the way, I read the article in NYTimes and glimpsed at your blog and I must say that your lives are pretty impressive.

As you have been in Split two years ago, you probably know the layout of the city. Our apartment is located on the southern slopes of the Marjan Hill, ca. 20 minutes on foot from the western promenade and 30 minutes to the famous promenade Riva. The walk to the city centre is beautiful because it goes along the sea, passing by a park and the west bank with its restaurants, cafes and yachts. There is also a bus stop 50 m away from the apartment with a bus line directly to the main promenade. We also have bikes for our guests, free of charge.

A good-sized grocery store (with butcher, bakery products, fruits and vegetables) is a 15-minute walk away, close-by are also a post office (also exchange office), ATM machine, pharmacy, newspaper kiosk, park, hairdresser...

I will be happy to take you to the grocery store when you come, so you can do some larger initial shopping for the first time and do not have to carry it back to the apartment.

The neighborhood we are located in and our street are a very popular area, where even residents and tourists from other parts of the city come to spend time, because it is very nice. A lovely pebble beach is just below the apartment.

Regarding the price of the apartment, I would like to point out that we already provide a 5% discount for weekly stays to our guests.

If you decide to stay at our house, we will be happy to be your hosts and assist and help wherever we can, even before you get here. So, I hope I answered your questions as much as possible. If there is anything else you'd like to know, please do not hesitate to contact me.

Best regards from sunny Split, Jelena
Split, Croatia 2016

Once we've booked our new home, we use the Airbnb's automatic response to notify the other hosts that we have chosen another rental. However, if we've exchanged more than a few emails with a host, we also send a personal note of thanks because we respect the time it takes a host to manage their listings and we encourage them to continue to be responsive and welcoming to all inquiries.

Enzo knew every inch of Bari.

Given our approach to finding our next home, it might look like we've made the process more complicated than necessary. After all, we could just look for Superhosts or use Instant Book. While we always look at all Superhost listings, we avoid the filter because we want to support fledgling hosts when we can, and we might miss gems in the rough like Jelena and Sanne. As for Instant Book, it has its advantages, of course, but we enjoy the back and forth with potential hosts before we book, especially since we no longer have a home other than our next Airbnb – so not only do we want to find a place we love, we want to find hosts who love what they do.

3

Finding Your Front Door
Getting there

"Not all those who wander are lost."

– J.R.R. Tolkien

When the reservation reminder arrives from Airbnb telling us to "pack our bags," Michael starts humming Willie Nelson's hit "On the Road Again," breaking into lyrics when he gets to ". . . Goin' places that I've never been, Seein' things that I may never see again . . . I can't wait to get on the road again," followed by more contented humming. This ritual goes on for a few days because the words ring true — we do like being on the road, seeing new places, and meeting new people. Just like Willie on tour, it's time to knock down the set, stow the gear, pack the bags, and hit the road.

Ready to take on Travel Day.

This is our Travel Day, as we call it, when we leave one Airbnb in the morning and hopefully arrive at the next by dinner time. Transportation might include a bus, a train, or an airplane. More than once it's been all three! While you're busy scrubbing the bathroom, fluffing the pillows, chilling the drinks (hint), and making sure your place lives up to the description on Airbnb's website, we're doing our best to get there and we can't wait to meet you. But we're also a little apprehensive. Did we make the right choice? Can we find your place?

Preparation for Travel Day actually begins several days earlier with an email to our next host. This is where our guest experience really begins – well before we arrive at your front door. The host who is engaged and goes the extra mile to make sure our stay matches our expectations quickly changes from host to friend.

After reconnecting to say "hello! Remember us?" Michael shares our arrival information and gets instructions on the best way to find our host's listing from the bus, train station, or the airport. He takes great care with his correspondence with hosts. He labors over the emails and works especially hard to get accurate information about directions and expectations at the arrival end – including the all-important contact number for phone and text messages. When I tease him about his multiple spreadsheets and obsessive planning, he reminds me that "just like painting a house, success lies in the prep work." Besides, he huffs, he is quite certain our hosts appreciate his careful attention to detail.

Most often the host responses and directions are straightforward – just how Michael likes them, and I leave it to him to find the address when we hit the ground. However, when we do navigate together, it can get a little fractious. He prefers GPS and I like a paper map. He enjoys clear direction while I don't mind scanning for visual clues (note: it never hurts to add "take the next right just past the small shop with the blue awning" to your otherwise clear directions). He threw up his hands when we got these directions from our host in Andorra, but I found them to be an intriguing challenge:

> Hello Michael, ...you have about 20 minutes of walking...When you arrive you must get a plan à the station of when you are on the street turn on your left and walk until the main street, turn right ...you have to go up to Escaldes ask first for the main street "Avenida Carlemany ..." And up to Escaldes to the credit andorra ....on your left you will have a bank color green " crédit Andorra " when you arrived there you turn left, you walk 250 m always on left ...you pass the river and you are there ...on your left you have a small' supermarket and a shop "Balduffa " for babies ...you take a small passage beside Balduffa and at the end turn left it's the Bloc À. Then there are the doors. I hope it's clear for you .... Have a good trip.
>
> See you soon - Monique
> Andorra, April 2016

Okay, maybe a bit *too* challenging even for me. After a few false starts we decided to take a taxi – but even our driver was a little confused and called for help. Our host met us outside the building as we arrived, and we had a delightful stay with our new friends in a beautiful mountain setting.

I'm a little hard on maps.

When you share bus or metro details, including how and where to catch them, we declare our undying love for you. Even though we've hauled ourselves and our bags onto just about every form of transportation there is, it's always a challenge – especially in a new city. A great deal of that stress is removed by your guidance. Here's a great example from our host in Tel Aviv:

Hi Michael how are you? I checked the trains. There is a train leaving from the airport at 19:35 and another train leaving at 20:05. It depends when you land... take the train from the airport to Tel Aviv Haganah station, and from there you take a taxi. 12-minute train and a 15-minute taxi. Tickets for the train costs 16 nis each. The price for a taxi depending on the time she arrives (40-50 nis). The train is less comfortable but cheaper than direct taxi to Tel Aviv (180 nis). There is in the train station stairs but I can not know if it is a problem for you. I hope I explained well, and you understand me :). I would love to help if you have any more questions.

Regards, Arbel
Tel Aviv, April 2015

Similarly, our host in Rome sent us perfect instructions. An email like this one would be helpful in any city, but it gave us particular confidence in such a huge, bustling metropolis:

Dear Michael and Debbie, about your arrival, you have two different options: The first one is less expensive, but - of course - a bit longer: From Fiumicino you can get the Leonardo Express to Rome Termini (about 30 minutes). The train costs 14 euros per person each way. From Termini get the metro Line A (direction Battistini) and get off at Cipro. From the Cipro tube station the flat is about 5 minutes walking. In total it will take you about 1 hour and half. The secondo one is faster but more expensive: From Fiumicino you can get a taxi (always get the regular ones, which are the white taxi); the fixed cost is 48 euros and it takes about 20-25 minutes. I do not recommend, however, to get a taxi from Termini station as the cost of the train + the cost of the taxi (about 12-15 euros from Termini to the flat) would be almost equal to what you might spend in a taxi from Fiumicino!! Let me know if you need any further information!

Best, Fede
Rome, March 2014

Travel Day starts by packing our trusty suitcases. Usually we carry 23 kilos (50 pounds) in each bag. When we travel by air, we slim down to meet most discount airline weight limits of 20kg (44 pounds) or risk being charged sky-high fees for every extra kilo. Out with the olive oil, the wine, and a book or two – they are now at the house we just left. During a flight on Ryanair from Paris to Porto, Portugal, we were slightly over the weight limit and hoped the airline would look the other way. But no, they turned out to be particularly strict – not only on the weight but also the limit of one carry-on per person. We had to step out of line and re-jig our checked luggage right there on the floor in front of the counter (one of our more embarrassing travel experiences). We each threw on two coats, stuffed our pockets, and jammed our daypacks to their maximum capacity – and that included stuffing my purse inside my daypack since that counted as a carry-on.

Our daypacks were so heavy at that point they could have easily flipped us on our backs with one false step; and we looked like rank amateurs at security. To avoid those comical scenarios in the future, we now have a firm no-purchase policy. If you can't eat it, drink it, attend it, or get somewhere on it, don't

Counting every kilo.

buy it. If you absolutely must have a new pair of shoes (and who doesn't?) one pair must be left behind. The same goes for T-shirts and toiletries. And we don't even consider souvenirs. However, one of the challenges of year-round travel is packing for a wide range of climates and activities. And that equals big suitcases that can stretch to accommodate whatever goes inside like an elastic waistband at an all-you-can-eat buffet. I'm constantly compelled to explain to our hosts, taxi drivers, and anyone else who handles our cumbersome bags that we travel full time. They don't care. They've already decided we are crazy Americans and I must have 20 pairs of shoes in my suitcase.

After three years of constantly moving from place to place, we realize much can happen on Travel Day that is outside our control. Therefore our rules on Travel Day include a commitment to stay married, at least for that day; be kind to each other, be flexible, tolerant, and definitely apply the "If you can't say something nice, better to say nothing at all" rule. These maxims have served us well throughout our marriage of 38 years, but on a day where we could be on the road for many hours using multiple forms of transportation in any number of languages, they are imperative. We have yet to see how "I can't *believe* we're heading in the absolute wrong direction from the airport on an express train that doesn't stop for another 45 minutes!" shouted at the person who said "I think this is our train" gets you anywhere. Certainly not to the airport. That actually happened in Barcelona and it made for a stressful and expensive cab ride back. But we shook it off and made our flight.

Any time is game time.

For budgetary reasons, we prefer using public transportation or walking from the station if it's close. But if that means tons of stairs (Paris Metro) or a long, bone-rattling walk on cobbled streets (Granada, Spain) with our rolling bags and heavy packs, we'll splurge for a taxi. I have enough taxi stories, good and bad, to fill a chapter, but that's for another book. Approaching a driver, knowing the fare you told us "not to pay a penny over," is a great negotiating tool. We watch the greedy light in the driver's eyes fade as he realizes we had local information and weren't the gullible tourists he'd hoped for.

When we arrive in a new city, we have three priorities. Find SIM cards for our phones, find transportation to your Airbnb, and connect with you. In order to communicate in any given country, we need to have a short-term phone plan with data. Michael could give a Ted Talk on how to get SIM cards anywhere in the world. It's something you don't think about when traveling within your own country, especially America, or even on vacation to a foreign country. But when we cross international borders, we need a SIM card for each new country. So far we've each had 50 different phone numbers, but more importantly, data plans that allow for calling, texting, and Internet access. We may roam, but our phones *may* not.

When we're unable to find SIM cards right away, we scout for an approachable local, usually a young person who hopefully speaks English, and politely ask him or her to call you to tell you we've arrived. Michael, our Chief Travel Planner, has all of your contact information in his phone and on a piece of paper in his wallet in case one or the other gets lost. He's even loaded the information in Google Translate into the language of our destination country the night before we leave in case our taxi driver doesn't speak English. Michael can hand him the phone with the following message: "*Please take us to this address and would you please call this number and let our Airbnb host know we are on our way? Thank you!*" Sometimes the driver is puzzled, and maybe even a little reluctant, but so far it's worked and we breathe a great sigh of relief when we hear you pick up on the other end.

One time, and one time only, Michael decided he didn't need to go to these extremes. And that was a lesson learned. We'd just arrived in the seaside town of Essaouira, Morocco, after a jarring five-hour bus trip from Marrakesh. As we stepped off the bus in a desolate, dusty bus station parking lot, we were immediately swarmed by "helpful" young men offering taxis, old men with rickety push-carts hoping to carry our bags, and guides hawking camel rides and hotel discounts. Add a few hangers-on and you've got a show! This was the first time in our Nomadic travels that we didn't have exact contact information for our host on paper or in Michael's phone. Perhaps it was because our host told us, "It's a small town, just grab a cab and give the driver the name of my restaurant. It should cost about 10 dirham" (about a dollar). After a lot of animated discussion and grabbing at Michael's iPhone to verify this information, there was confusion about the location of the restaurant because there was one with a similar name inside the Medina where taxis cannot go (that got the cart guys excited!). Finally we found our host Federico because, thank God, we had Moroccan SIM cards and could call the restaurant. We thrust the phone at a cab driver and hoped for the best. After a brief discussion with our host, the deal was done and the crowd moved on.

Regardless of the way you provide directions, it always helps if you've described your front door or the building entrance since that's what we'll be looking for.

The entrance to our flat in Larnica.

After a long day of travel from Berlin, we were hot and tired when we finally reached our destination in Milan. Or so we thought. The taxi was long gone and we were left staring at 12-foot tall, highly polished wooden doors with two menacing lion head door knockers. Nice place. Probably too nice. We knocked a few times and waited. And waited. No answer. This was only our fifth Airbnb so we were not yet the calm, collected travelers we are today. We frantically accosted a stranger and implored him to use his cellphone to call our host and describe where we were. It turned out we had been dropped on the right street just several doors from our more modest abode because we had written the house number incorrectly. Had we known we were looking for a red gate tucked in from the street, we probably could have figured it out.

One of our favorite front doors was a hatch. We rented a sailboat in La Grazie, Italy, and were looking forward to living aboard for a few days. We miss the sailboat we sold back in Seattle to help finance this adventure, and even though we wouldn't be leaving the marina, we welcomed the chance to be on the water. Our host's father, a salty old sea dog of few words, met us at the nearest bus stop. After a gruff welcome, he grabbed both our big bags by the handle and took off down the street, leaving us scampering to keep up. A few quick turns later, we left the village behind and followed him single file down a very long, narrow dirt path that occasionally offered a glimpse of the sea through gaps in the overgrown vegetation. After breaking into a clearing, we saw the marina below us. We maneuvered our luggage down three flights of steep wooden stairs and then along the dock to our Airbnb boat. Getting our bags onboard across the wobbling gangplank was the last challenge. But after that it was smooth sailing – just without the sailing.

Having opened just about every kind of front door, we now realize the condition of the exterior of a building doesn't nec-

Our floating front door.

essarily reflect what's waiting for us inside. In many countries, the economy is finally showing signs of recovery and hosts have been able to purchase a flat and turn it into wonderful living space – but they often can't do anything about the crumbling, sometimes graffiti-covered conditions of their building. This became especially true as we traveled deeper into Eastern Europe. There, Airbnb apartments become more "interesting." That's the word our eldest daughter Kelly uses when she doesn't want to offend – such as, "Mom, this new soup you made tonight is interesting," (meaning, you don't need to make it again). In the case of our apartment in Bucharest, Romania, interesting began at the entrance. When the taxi pulled up, we thought there must be a mistake because we'd stopped in front of an Erotica Shopping Mall. But no, the address was correct. Our jovial host popped out of a small door next to a sex shop to welcome us and help carry our luggage upstairs. For the rest of the week we furtively came in and out of our latest front door.

Our X-rated front door.

In Riga, Latvia, we were hesitant to enter a building complex that looked unsafe. To access it, we had to walk through a few sketchy passageways, skirt overflowing dumpsters, and navigate a smelly, dark stairway. But once our delightful host opened the door and welcomed us inside, we discovered the very modern, stylish apartment that matched the photos in the listing. If we hadn't trusted Airbnb and the description, we would have missed the opportunity to stay in a beautiful home with an expansive view over the city. That happened a number of times — so now when we arrive at a building that gives us pause, we bravely cross the threshold because we know it's what's on the inside that counts.

Several times you've met us with your car, or helped us with our luggage from the train or bus station to your Airbnb. Having you, or a trusted surrogate, meet us for this last leg of our journey is one of the nicest welcomes we could ask for. It shows you feel personally responsible for our comfort and safety, and it's a great way to learn more about you and your city as we head home together.

Although in Helsinki we thought we might not make it home. Our host, Riitta, met us at the airport with her car. She was a bundle of energy, and her spiky mop of orange hair suited her well. She hustled us to the parking garage, filling us in on details about her neighborhood and city, occasionally stopping to breathe. The luggage was a tight fit in her battered red sedan, even with me squeezed in the back with whatever didn't fit in the trunk. Michael sat up front with his knees pressed against the glove box. After several tries, Riitta was able to find reverse on her manual transmission and bolted out of the parking space. From there it was a page straight from "Mr. Toad's Wild Ride."

Both Michael and I are familiar with manual transmissions — Michael was a professional race car driver at one time, and

I had loved shifting through the gears of my butter-yellow Volkswagen convertible, so we were fully aware that Riitta had *no* idea how to drive this car. There were shuddering stops, grinding gears, agonizing starts from 2nd gear, and a general disregard for signals and signage. Both Michael and I desperately wanted to ask her to pull over so one of us could drive, but being overly polite to a fault, we white-knuckled it the entire way with just the occasional gasp until we literally hit the curb in front of her house.

Travel Day takes its toll on us, and that is probably true for anyone, especially those traveling in a foreign country who are no doubt bewildered and jet-lagged. Add to that the challenge of finding a private home with a quirky address as opposed to a hotel, and not knowing what, or who, is waiting for us on the other side of the door. There is little doubt you're going to have a frazzled guest on your hands. You are the person, the new friend, who can make or break our experience right from the moment you say "Hello." When we meet you for the first time, and you are warm and welcoming, we don't care about the front of your building, or that a wide-angle lens made your place look twice the size — or even if you forgot to mention you have four cats — we are just happy to be safe, and finally home.

4

Anybody Home?
We hope you are

"I got gaps; you got gaps;
we fill each other's gaps."

— Rocky

At several airports, banks, grocery stores, and even a dentist's office once, we've seen simple instant survey systems at the exit featuring four large buttons indicating your level of satisfaction with the service. The buttons ranged from a very sad red face to a very happy yellow face.

We know Airbnb is keen on the 5-star system but, if we were using this rating system to score how we feel about who greets us when we arrive, it would go as follows:

The keys are next door at the pizza restaurant and you can't be found

A property manager shows up to hand over the keys and offers a quick rundown of the basics

A trusted friend or family member greets us, knows all about the place, and describes where things are and how they work

You are there to welcome us personally and show us how to make ourselves comfortable in your home and in your neighborhood

We've had so many big happy button experiences that we can't begin to share them all — and fortunately we've rarely pressed the disappointed frowning face.

One of our favorite Airbnbs in Paris is owned by Gaelle, an engaging host who lives in Senegal. Obviously, she couldn't be in Paris to meet us but her affable brother showed up to greet us. On our second visit, her best friend welcomed us back. Both were familiar with the flat and the area and were easy to reach by phone and text if necessary. Gaelle even went so far as to check in on us by email several times during our stays. Because the flat is close to our daughter's home, we've also made some great family memories at Gaelle's place and consider it our home in Paris.

Making memories in Paris.

In Edinburgh, our host Dario was called out of town at the last minute but his delightful parents met us. They were very proud to show off their son's apartment and even more proud to tell us all about their dear Dario. The only thing this special young man seemed to lack was a wife – and thus grandchildren were a long way off. Did we perhaps know any lovely American girls who might be interested in moving to Scotland?

In Ljubljana, our host Irene knew we would be arriving May 1st and, as Americans, we might not realize it was an important national holiday where everything is shut tighter than on Christmas morning. No three-day Blowout Sales around here. In fact, many shops remain *closed* for three days. She thoughtfully filled the fridge with lifesaving provisions that included cold cuts, cheese, beer, bread and chocolate as well as ample breakfast fixings for the next morning.

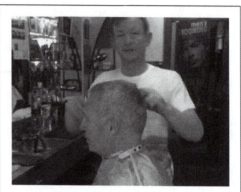
Haircut on the house in Dublin.

We found a great Airbnb in Dublin in an area called Temple Bar. The pictures were wonderful, the location central, and we looked forward to our week there. Our host Alan loaded the kitchen with snacks and beverages and even gave Michael a free haircut in his family's historic barbershop on the ground floor of the building. This largess could possibly have been to make up for the fact that, unbeknownst to us, we were perched above one of the loudest bars in Dublin with live music and drunken sing-alongs well into the night. Maybe we should have taken a hint from the word "Bar" in Temple Bar. In the spirit of "if you can't beat them, join them," we found some fine Irish pubs and while we didn't sing along, we hoisted a brew or two.

Country life in County Wexford.

During our stay in a 300-year-old postcard-perfect farmhouse in County Wexford, the only singing was provided by songbirds. Our hosts, Eoin and Sharon, couldn't meet us (they were expecting a baby at any minute in Dublin) but Mary Elisabeth Doyle, the sweetest, rosy-cheeked grandmother you could conjure from any storybook, came up the long drive to welcome us. Over her arm was a basket filled with warm, homemade scones and a jar of her special strawberry jam. She enjoyed filling us in on daily life in Wexford and nearby Barntown and expected to see us down the lane at St. Alphonsus Church on Sunday. We were there.

In Trinidad, Cuba, our host Kiwi had arranged for a taxi to meet us at the central bus station so, thankfully, we were able to avoid the pack of drivers swarming our bus looking for a fare. We piled into his rattletrap Russian Lada (my door was wired shut with a coat hanger), and with Elton John blaring at top volume we made our way out of the crowded city center and then down a narrow dirt road to the tiny beach town of La Boca, where he dropped us at a modest stone bungalow.

There we were greeted by our congenial host, her mother, her cousin, and her five-year-old niece who quickly attached herself to my side. Oh, and a dog, a cat, a parrot, and about 40 chickens including a rooster, and several hens with chicks of all ages that were "free range" to the point they would wander into your room if you didn't keep the door closed.

Once inside our room, we took one look at the flamingo-pink walls and purple satin bedding and decided we needed a few minutes to recuperate and adjust to our "interesting" new quarters. So we headed to the small courtyard to have a drink and read for a while. It was then that Michael realized he had left his Kindle on the bus! This was cause for alarm because here we were, in what seemed the middle of nowhere, billeted in a hot-pink bedroom with little to do beyond reading our backlog of books and play Scrabble.

An indifferent host, or poor surrogate, could have easily ignored this bit of personal drama. But Kiwi jumped into action.

Our youngest host in Trinidad, Cuba.

She called our taxi driver, who was back in Trinidad by that time, and asked for help. He rushed to the bus station and, luckily, found our bus and driver. They both searched the bus but couldn't find the Kindle. Truth be told, we weren't entirely convinced they knew what they were looking for. In desperation, we asked Kiwi to call the driver again to pick us up so that we could return to the bus station and look for it ourselves. It was a tense ride. Michael was as frustrated as I've ever seen him, especially since he was two-thirds through a great book and there would be no way to replace a Kindle until we left Cuba two weeks later.

Fortunately, the bus was still there, but it was fully loaded with the engine idling and ready for imminent departure. The driver was reluctant to have his bus rummaged through again, but we were determined. We searched our seats and the surrounding areas and even questioned the passengers, but still no

Kindle. In the end, all we could do was file a useless Lost Property Report. As I was filling out the form, Michael decided to search one last time because, once the bus left, that would be the end of the story. Suddenly, I heard a whoop and looked up to see him with his Kindle held high! Because it has a dark blue cover, and the bus seats were blue, no one noticed it had slipped sideways between our two seats. Kiwi was thrilled to have been able to help and had fresh Mojitos ready when we returned home. She was more than our host. She was our hero.

Michael and I usually rent an entire house wherever we stay. In fact, we've only shared a room in a house three times, and then for very short stays, except in Cuba where it's customary to live with your hosts in their homes. So, on nearly every occasion, once we've met our hosts and had our orientation, they wave goodbye and we are blissfully on our own. But in Prague we weren't so sure that would be the case.

During our pre-arrival email sessions, our host Hana invited us to have dinner with them at the apartment on our arrival day. She was looking forward to making a traditional Hungarian goulash and we were eager for an authentic home-cooked meal. She and her husband Lukas were there to greet us at the front door around four o'clock in the afternoon. We sat in the living room and began to get to know each other. Soon it was time for them to collect their two small children from daycare and make a quick stop at the store. Michael and I went for a walk in the park nearby and returned to find them back with 4-year-old Lola and her 9-month-old baby brother Alfred. I had discreetly looked around the kitchen earlier but didn't see any dinner preparations underway, nor did I see bags packed for their departure. But before long we were playing with the kids and I didn't give it another thought. Hana got dinner ready for the kids and we helped feed them. Eventually Hana began to prepare our dinner, which I worried would take us late into the evening and surely it was getting to be past bedtime for the little ones. Finally, Michael took me aside and quietly asked, "Did we make a mistake in our booking? Are we sharing a

Time to say goodbye!

room here?" I didn't think so, but the way things were going, they wouldn't be leaving much before 9:00 p.m., *if* they were leaving. And we were getting anxious to unpack and settle in.

At the risk of sounding crazy, I had to ask what the evening held in store. As it turned out, Hana had prepared dinner the day before so the most delicious goulash we'd ever tasted just needed reheating and was soon on the table with steamed potatoes and a simple salad. The kids were happily playing in their pajamas and, like most European kids, stay up much later than we are used to. And finally, we learned the family bags were all packed and in the car. Yes, they laughed, they would be leaving to stay at Hana's parents for the week as soon as the dishes were done. We were quick to offer to do the dishes. In fact, we said Michael *loves* doing dishes, and under no circumstance would we hear otherwise. "Thank you for the wonderful dinner – now you just get yourselves on the road before you are too tired to drive. Off you go! Bye now!" We gently pushed our lovely host family out the door and nearly collapsed on the kitchen floor.

After staying in more than a hundred Airbnbs, we know this extraordinary type of hospitality isn't easy on either side of the door. We appreciate how difficult it must be to maintain the high standards you've set, day after day, as you welcome new guests and respond cheerfully to their needs and expectations. We only hope you realize that for all of us weary travelers who drop their bags at your doorstep, you've more than earned that big yellow smiley button.

5

Home Sweet *Your* Home
Settling in

"When preparing to travel,
lay out all your clothes and all your money.
Then take half the clothes and twice the money."

– Susan Heller

For us, arriving in a new city is like coming home because your front door is our front door. We've dropped our bags and we feel like we can walk in, put the kettle on, put our feet up, and sit back and watch TV. Just like home.

However, on our first night in Naples in April 2014 Michael found me standing forlornly in the kitchen with tears running down my cheeks because I couldn't find a few key utensils I needed to make dinner.

This was our 50th kitchen and, looking back, I think I was suffering from a case of "Where am I?" I swear I saw a vegetable peeler. No wait, that was two weeks ago in Granada. I'd carried my favorite paring knife in my checked bag for six months, but recently I'd made the mistake of packing it in our "lunch kit" for a flight and it was snatched at security. As for a cheese grater, that's where I "lost it." I was in Italy. How could there be no cheese grater?

It had also been a long day of travel from Paris. We'd dragged our bags through the Metro, dealt with Easy Jet (not so easy), and, just as we arrived by bus from the Naples airport to the main terminal in the city, the skies darkened and a heavy spring downpour hit. Fortunately we found a taxi driver willing to take us to our Airbnb, or so we thought. The apartment was tucked away in the tangle of alleyways and narrow streets that make up the city's Spanish Quarter. After a few attempts to find it, our exasperated driver declared he was "fini!" We put up some resistance, followed by pleading, so he begrudgingly called our hosts from his cellphone to tell them where he'd dropped us. He then sped off leaving us like ransom victims being returned to their family by the Mafia.

As it turned out we were just a couple of blocks from our Airbnb. Our host Francesco and his teenage son Gabrielle dashed through the rain to welcome us and gather our luggage for the short sprint back to the front door of the building. We still had five flights of twisting medieval stairs to navigate so we were grateful for their help. Once inside, Francesco's wife Elisabetta started fussing over us with big fluffy towels and had coffee brewing. We knew then we were in good hands with the Moribito family.

After we'd dried off and gathered around the table, we learned more about our neighborhood and how things worked in our new home. We'd read that the neighborhood was in a dangerous part of the city but Francesco assured us it was safe. As we went over the city map he showed us the areas to avoid after dark, just like in any big city. Elisabetta circled the markets she trusted for good produce and best prices, and their favorite and most affordable restaurants. Meanwhile, Michael started an animated conversation with Francesco about how to buy tickets for the SSC Napoli vs. Milan football match later in the week. Gabrielle spoke the best English and tried his best to interpret during our fast-moving conversations, but there

Fresh vegetables outside our door in Naples.

were still dramatic hand gestures, constant interruptions, flashing translator screens, and a lot of laughter.

I had been fantasizing about cooking in Italy for weeks and, armed with Elisabetta's recommendations, I was ready. When the sun made a brief appearance, I rushed out to scour the neighborhood for minestrone ingredients and returned with my shopping bags near to bursting just before the next squall blew through. Soon the counter was overflowing with dirt-specked carrots and potatoes, stalks of celery, juicy tomatoes, onions, garlic, fragrant oregano, fresh basil, cannelloni beans, fat sausages, and a prize chunk of golden Parmigiano-Reggiano.

I set about cooking in what I was certain was my dream kitchen because, after all, we were in Italy – isn't every Italian kitchen stocked with everything you need to whip up Mario Batali's favorite weeknight dinner? But in our rush in from the rain, and my haste to shop before the next storm, I hadn't inspected the cupboards and drawers. Usually that's the first thing I do. I have to say, most everything I hoped for was on hand – except those three missing kitchen essentials.

When Michael saw my face he knew swift action was the only remedy. Even though the rain had come back with a vengeance, he turned into "Super Nomad" and volunteered to find the missing utensils that had brought me to tears. My hero. I quickly sketched what I was looking for so he wouldn't have translation issues and off he went. He returned a short while later, dripping wet but with the goods. He'd found a little souvenir shop where they sold all three items, complete with cute little carved vegetable handles. They weren't exactly what you'd pick out at your favorite cookware store, but they did the job and the soup was delicious.

My most treasured souvenirs.

Every two weeks or so we set out to explore a new city, often in a different country. By the time we arrive at our next Airbnb we have a pretty good sense of the city from our own research. But it is you, our host, who makes the real difference in our experience during our stay. Just like in Naples, you welcome us into your home, review the map with us while sharing your favorite restaurants and shops, point out what not to miss while we're there, and describe how to use public transportation. You also show us how the TV remotes work (never enough times) and how to use the washing machine. At this point we know a little more about each other, the neighborhood, and our new home. We appreciate your sincere, "If you need anything please let us know." But after we hug, or kiss, or shake hands depending on the customs of the country, we close the door behind you, shut our eyes, and take a deep breath.

Alone in our new home – your home – is the moment the two of us catch each other's eye and either break into a smile and do a little happy dance, or adjust to reality. Either way, it's still a first impression and we need to figure out how your home really works.

I head straight to the kitchen. Because we cook most of our meals at home, the kitchen gets the most scrutiny. No sense planning a pasta dinner if the biggest pot in the kitchen is just right for warming a can of soup. It's always interesting to discover what a host considers "everything you need to cook your own meals." Sometimes that's little more than what you'd find in a hiker's backpack while other times I feel like I am on the set of a television cooking show.

In some kitchens, the food cupboards are stuffed to the edge with remnants from the owner or past guests or – happy dance again – filled by our host with the basics, along with local specialties, spices, and good olive oil. The same is true with the fridge. It isn't appetizing to open the door to discover wilted vegetables, half-opened packages of lunch meat, and milk of a certain age. Personally, we are happy to find a clean, empty fridge but we always welcome a bottle of water and a couple of local beers. And ice! We don't count on it but it's always a treat. Having coffee, tea, milk, and sugar must be on the top of Airbnb's how-to-be-a-good-host list because it's rare we don't find those basics. If there's a bottle of wine as a gift, we are pleasantly surprised. But please be sure there's a wine opener (spoken from experience).

In Jerusalem, we were fortunate to find a beautiful apartment in the Jewish Quarter of the Old City during Passover. When we arrived, our delightful hosts, Yishai and Rivka, greeted us with tea and unleavened sweet bread. Yishai then shared with me the unique situation in our kitchen. "We offer two complete sets of dishes and utensils to choose from," he explained. He pointed to the large, comprehensively stocked kosher cupboard, and another almost equally well-stocked cup-

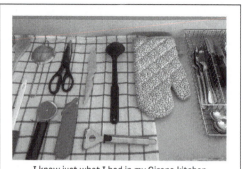
I knew just what I had in my Girona kitchen.

board for those who don't keep kosher. Yishai explained, "Either can be used, but the dishes should never be combined." Naturally there were a few items I coveted from the kosher side that weren't on my side. I'm not sure if what happened next is, well, "kosher" but Yishai said that since no one had used any of the kosher dishes, he could move the few items I couldn't live without to our side with the stern admonishment they were not to be moved back. It was one of my favorite kitchen experiences.

While I am exploring the kitchen, Michael has his own checklist. He sets up the WiFi and the charging station for our phones and laptops, and then, if we haven't gotten them already, sources where to get SIM cards for our phones. He checks the lights, tests the bed, runs the shower, double-checks the keys and locks (those have a personality of their own), and flips through the house manual if there is one. We are always grateful when there is. In Paris, if our host hadn't noted that the kitchen light switch was awkwardly located behind the refrigerator, and the best way to reach it was with the handle of the wooden spoon he kept on the counter just for that purpose, we would have been left in the dark.

Because we will be living in our Airbnb just as we live at home, we also start "setting up house." Ideally there are drawers for our clothes, a shelf in the bathroom, and an empty kitchen cupboard for our food. We fluff our pillows, get out the candles, put on our music, and place our books by the bedside. Maybe we'll start a load of laundry. Then we set up

Our Marrakesh mini-kitchen.

our work area — that's where a big table comes in. It is one of the things on our list of criteria when searching for a home because we tend to spread out with our computers to do our writing, play games, and of course eat all that food I prepare. Add a fast wireless Internet connection and we are all set.

We read a lot. It's affordable and enjoyable and our Amazon Kindles have been a godsend. Reading in bed at night is part of our routine and that's why reading lights on both sides of the bed are always appreciated — especially if we have treated ourselves to paper books. But sometimes there *are* no sides of the bed. In Vienna our bed was comfortable but stuffed into an alcove with less than an inch on either side. It seemed romantic in the pictures, but depending on your definition of romantic, getting tucked in meant approaching the head of the bed like a bear on all fours.

Every host has his or her own style and ways of making a guest feel at home. More often than not, it's the little things that make a big difference. Wendy in Amsterdam left us with an overflowing basket of regional treats. Hande in Izmir topped up Michael's cellphone as a surprise. Laura in Parma keeps a huge pad of tear-off maps from the tourism office and, over coffee, she circles her favorite places on the front and then writes personal recommendations that fit each guest's interests on the back. Our hosts in Brussels, Iria and Elsie, invited us to their flat for wine and appetizers (they hold private din-

The perfect bed for hibernation.

ner parties in their home) and then brought toys and treats over when our five-year-old granddaughter joined us for a week. In Chisinau, Moldova, our host didn't speak a word of English but his passionate briefing in Russian came through loud and clear in English over the speaker in his phone using an app called iTranslate Voice. Michael returned the favor and the two bonded over a political discussion via phone translation that ended with Putin-style bear hugs.

In nearly every city, our hosts have gone out of their way to make our stay exceptional. In fact, that seems to be the motivation behind opening their homes to strangers. We couldn't

Iria and Elsie fed us well in Brussels.

be more thankful because that is what motivates us as well —
meeting you and learning how to live in your city as a local,
just as you do.

6

We Belong
Living like a local

"There are no foreign lands.
It is the traveler only who is foreign."

– Robert Louis Stevenson

Michael and I first visited Greece in the spring of 2014 when teams around the world were in the final stages of qualifying for the upcoming World Cup in Brazil. While there, we learned that Greece would be playing a do-or-die match in Athens just a few miles from our Airbnb. Michael, an avid football fan, was determined to be there. All he needed was a ticket.

Our host Vassili jumped into action. Not only did he find a difficult-to-get ticket for Michael, he snagged one for himself as well so they could go together even though he isn't a football fan. As if that wasn't enough, he wouldn't let Michael pay

Michael and Vassili heading out in Athens.

for his ticket. On the night of the match we had dinner with Vassili and his wife Helena at their favorite restaurant. During the evening we discovered many common interests around EU politics, culture, food and wine. And now, of course, European football. Michael has managed to attend over 24 matches in a dozen countries during our travels. But this match was early in our trip and he was beyond excited. After dinner, the boys threw on their coats, paid the bill, and raced off on Vaselli's motorcycle heading down the motorway at 70 mph to the stadium, reaching their seats just in time for the Greek National Anthem. To top it off, Greece prevailed and qualified for the World Cup. It was a truly memorable evening for Michael thanks to a host who went above and beyond the call of hospitality.

As we continued our travels, we were eager to watch World Cup matches wherever we were staying because we had a very competitive family pool going. But during our stay in Helsinki, we discovered our host Riitta didn't own a television. When we realized we'd be unable to watch qualifying matches (many of which started after midnight) we were devastated. How would we follow our teams? Riitta to the rescue. She found the official website streaming matches online and hooked Michael's laptop up to her LCD projector. We were all set and could watch the action into the wee hours of the night on our kitchen wall – just like being in a sports bar!

Many hosts may think their job is done once we've shut the door behind them, and offer little or no further contact until it's time to say goodbye. But good hosts like Vassili, Helena and Riitta and those I mentioned in the previous chapter are

A farmhouse lunch in Slovenia.

the ones who know how to create a 5-star guest experience by continuing to provide hospitality throughout their guests' stay. That doesn't mean hovering, or constantly engaging with guests. But it does mean being available for questions, offering assistance as problems arise, and helping guests explore their city in ways that allow them to truly feel part of it.

Some of our hosts have even gone the extra mile to reduce the stress that comes with trying to do "normal" things in a foreign country – situations like making dental and doctor appointments. In Bari, our host Enzo's wife was a pharmacist and helped fill a much-needed prescription. Our host Wendy in Wales arranged a hair appointment for me with her favorite hairdresser. Elsie, our host in Brussels, even went so far as to walk me to the best toy store in town to purchase a birthday present for our grandson, and then took me to the post office to help with the customs' paperwork. Jelena, our host in Split, arranged an interview with the local paper about our travels. And in Antwerp, our host Isabelle's father drove Michael 10 miles out of town to collect a FedEx package at the airport. It's these extra efforts that make you feel like you have more than a host – you have a good neighbor.

Often we simply spent time with our hosts, exchanging stories about each other's lives, customs and cultures. Jelena described raising a family in post-conflict Croatia as we sat over coffee in a café along the Riva in Split. In Florence, I had fun carving a Halloween pumpkin for our host's children. In Zadar, Croatia, I spent an early morning up on a ladder with our host Elza picking cherries in the back garden. During our stay in Pézenas, France, I was able to surprise our host Louisa by baking a loaf of banana bread in her fabulous kitchen for her birthday. And in Havana, Michael sat on the front porch with our elderly host Evelio sipping cold beer and talking politics. One of Michael's favorite questions is, "If you had a magic wand, what would you wish for?" Michael told me afterward that he had indeed asked Evelio that question, but with a Cuban twist. He wanted to know that if Evelio magically became the president of Cuba, replacing Raúl Castro, what changes he would make. Michael anticipated a lengthy list of reforms, but instead was surprised to hear that Evelio could not even begin to imagine becoming the ruler of Cuba and, even if he was he wasn't sure there was a single thing he would change.

Michael was dumbfounded and concluded that a lifetime of controlled media had obviously had a profound impact. You don't get those experiences and insights every day.

Politics on the porch with Evelio.

We also benefit when hosts share similar interests. One morning, over Viennese coffee with our Salzburg hosts, Markus and Katrin, the conversation turned to classical music. The couple had two teenage sons, the youngest of whom was an accomplished pianist who attended the prestigious Mozart Universität near our Airbnb. Having learned of our love of classical music, they invited us to their son's recital the next evening. We were honored to be included with the rest of the family, and the performance by three young musicians was outstanding enough to have been performed on any stage in the world. If we hadn't met for coffee, we would never have had that experience, or discovered the dozens of other free performances of music, opera and theater on campus throughout the week.

People often ask us how we choose our destinations. I love museums and ancient history where Michael has a fascination with current events and 20th-century history. Many of the decisions about where we head next have to do with current politics which we both follow closely. The good news is that ancient, recent and current history run deep wherever we end up.

Michael has a particular interest in Eastern Europe and the ongoing challenges in that region. So that took us to Chisinau, Moldova, where our Russian host's daughter Tamara went above and beyond to make sure our stay was special. And she did it remotely from her home in Croatia.

Tamara was surprised, and delighted, to host Americans who were keen to learn about her native country. She went to work to be sure we had a good experience because there is very little in the way of organized tourism there. Not only did we exchange the usual flurry of emails, but she arranged two Skype video calls as well to be sure she fully understood what we wanted to accomplish, and then to share what she had planned for us. She organized a private city tour with an English-speaking guide, and a very special wine tasting at Cricova winery that included a photo of Michael standing next to Putin's private cave. The highlight was a guided day trip to Transnistria, a sliver of Europe caught between east and west in disputed territory along the Moldovan-Ukrainian border. Russia is firmly entrenched

Back in the U.S.S.R.

there, and with giant statues of Lenin, massive war memorials, the communist hammer and sickle symbol everywhere, and a few tanks for good measure, we felt we'd gone back in time to the heyday of the U.S.S.R. It's also not easy for westerners to visit this bizarre territory that, I might add, only Russia recognizes as a country. We knew Tamara wouldn't put us in danger, and we had a competent guide, so we thoroughly enjoyed the Cold War atmosphere, especially at the border crossing. However, no photos were allowed so I can't prove it.

In March 2015 we traveled from Turkey to the island of Cyprus. Michael wanted to learn more about the tug of war between Greece and Turkey over this rocky outpost in the Eastern Mediterranean. Personally, I never say no to an island. We landed on the Turkish side while our Airbnb was in the capital city of Nicosia, on the Greek side. Fortunately our gracious hosts, Paulo and Laura, arranged for a special taxi that had a license to travel between the two territories (not easy to get apparently). But that was just the beginning of their help in exploring this fascinating country. As we sat under the shade of the lemon tree in the beautiful courtyard that connected our house with theirs, we learned about their previous lives in Italy and the history of their adopted country of Cyprus.

Like the country, the city of Nicosia is also divided between Turkey and Greece. A heavily guarded border crossing cuts through the middle of the city center with armed guards overseen by UN Peacekeepers on both sides. Paulo and Laura invited us to walk to the Turkish side of the city for lunch to experience just what it's like to cross the border. We had to show our passports twice – once to the armed Cypriot guards, and again, about 50 feet down the street, to the guards on the Turkish side, with UN Peacekeepers watching the procedure. As obvious tourists we weren't questioned in detail, but it isn't as easy for locals to cross so we appreciated their will-

New friends Paulo and Laura.

ingness to make this unique experience possible. In fact, many Cypriots have never been to the Turkish side out of principle. We were able to see the differences between two cultures that live side-by-uncomfortable-side. For example, the Turkish side is poor, shabby, and not recognized as a country by anyone in the world besides Turkey, while the Greek side is polished, prosperous, part of the European Union, uses the Euro, and has been a member of the United Nations for over 50 years. We formed a great bond with these fellow global citizens who helped us better understand a complicated part of the world.

Living regional also means preparing local dishes whenever I can. In Marrakesh our Airbnb hosts offered housekeepers who stayed at your home during the day and prepare meals as requested – apparently a standard practice. I asked Rashida, the adorable young woman who looked after us in our first Riad, to teach me how to make a chicken tagine. She gladly took me shopping in the nearby souk to find the ingredients. Had I been alone, I'm certain I would have balked at entering the twisting alleyways filled with narrow shops and stalls overflowing with exotic elixirs, unfamiliar produce and conical pillars of spices – never mind dozens of donkey carts left double-parked and a crush of humanity.

We stopped at the spice markets and then haggled over vegetables – a process that even she couldn't explain. We bought too-hot-to-handle flat bread from a bakery that wasn't much more than a fire pit, and filled a bag full of rice from something that looked like a huge cow udder. Finally, the only item left on the list was the chicken. This turned out to be a very fresh chicken — as in lifted flapping and squawking from a crate filled with its brethren and dispatched before my very eyes. In under five minutes, it was plucked, hacked, wrapped, and in my basket. And I didn't faint. Together, Rashida and I made the most amazing chicken dish I've ever eaten. She also booked me into a cooking class with twelve other tourists who wanted to learn more about Moroccan cuisine. Part of the class time involved shopping for our ingredients and we were divided into three teams. I was anxious to demonstrate my newly acquired "local" knowledge and offered to take a few unsuspecting classmates to buy the chicken. Ha!

Making couscous the "right" way.

The culinary delights didn't end there. Our Marrakesh host Gilles invited us to join him for a special dinner, something he wouldn't normally extend to his Airbnb guests but we'd found a lot in common during our first meeting. He met us at the house and we meandered down several alleys until we arrived at a small wooden door – one that looked just like the dozens of other doors we'd passed. He knocked, and like a speakeasy, a small panel slid open revealing a pair of scrutinizing eyes. Gilles exchanged a few words with the gatekeeper and, with that, we entered a fragrant courtyard with trees draped in fairy lights and a fire blazing in a large hearth. It was a private dinner club where Gilles was a member. About a dozen other regulars and their guests were spread out on pillows by the fire or clustered under the trees deep in conversation. The chef owner served up a delicious, multi-course Mediterranean feast of whole roasted lamb with a fragrant couscous and flat breads for sopping up the juices. We dined well, drank well, and talked late into the night with people from all over the world, and spent about 20 USD for this unique experience.

During our trip to Madrid, our host, Enrique, did his utmost to make us happy and comfortable. First, he spent a great deal of time getting us settled and then personally took us around the neighborhood pointing out his favorite restaurants, bars, shops and sights. And, because it was two days before American Thanksgiving, he inquired on my behalf for a turkey (or parts of a turkey) whenever we passed a butcher. His perseverance was commendable, but we were out of luck. This would be the second year in a row that we couldn't find any traditional Thanksgiving ingredients. I don't hanker for American foodstuff very often, but Thanksgiving makes me a little homesick. The year before in Lisbon, we finally gave up and settled for mediocre Chinese food in a mostly deserted restaurant. I was hoping we could do better this year. Thanks to Enrique, we met a vendor at one of his favorite markets whose wife was American. Somehow his mother-in-law, who was in town, had procured a bird and they invited us to have Thanksgiving dinner with them. As if that weren't enough to start off the holiday season, Enrique went even further and used his skills as a professional photographer to take our picture for our 2014 Christmas card.

When we're not dining, cooking, exploring, or just spending time with our gracious hosts, we live just like everyone else. That includes enjoying the city. We budget for the "must see" attractions but also search for affordable cultural events, usually at churches and galleries. Just by walking a few miles each day, we've stumbled upon some of our most memorable free events, including The World Choir Games in Riga, Latvia; the first reading of a play in San Miguel de Allende, Mexico; 100 couples tango dancing in the Place de Catalunya in Barcelona; and scores of boisterous neighborhood festivals that seem to materialize out of nowhere. And we never miss a free walking tour where we learn so much about the local history and culture.

Try the free walking tour in your city.

Other than a brisk walk in the morning with a stop at a café or the market we can spend an entire day indoors just doing our banking online, making travel plans, booking our next Airbnb, catching up with friends and family, updating Facebook, Instagram, and our blog (and for several months, writing this book), and of course doing the laundry and cooking. We download books for our Kindles on Amazon or, better yet, free from the Seattle Public Library, and play a lot of games – Scrabble, backgammon, cribbage, and dominoes. And if we've figured out how the remotes work, we'll watch a little television, or NBC Nightly News on the iPad. Some of our hosts scratch their heads and wonder why we aren't out every day seeing the sights. But as our mantra reads: *we are living our daily lives just as we would at home, only in other peoples' houses around the world.* And just like any two people traveling

Sharing shortcake on the 4th of July.

together, we need time apart, even if it's just for an afternoon. So we always appreciate hosts who give us two sets of keys. That way I can go to a gallery and Michael can tour parliament and we don't have to worry about coordinating our schedules.

However we spend our days, they all seem to go by too quickly. So we're grateful for the exceptional hosts who help us get the most out of our stay. When you inquire about our interests and then suggest, or even accompany us to local events, we are so pleased. Because if it appealed to you, it will almost certainly appeal to us and once again allows us to feel a part of your community.

7

The Boy Scout Rule
How to be a Super Guest

"Travel has a way of stretching the mind.
The stretch comes not from travel's immediate
rewards, the inevitable myriad new sights,
smells and sounds, but with experiencing firsthand
how others do differently what we believed
to be the right and only way."

– Ralph Crawshaw

Twenty years ago Michael and I joined a sailing program in Seattle where boat owners shared their boats like landlubbers share condos in Palm Springs. Four families including us shared a beautiful Catalina 42' sailboat with her owner. Each partner could spend at least eight weeks a year aboard the *Pure Joy*. She definitely was a joy to sail, and our years on the water in the Pacific Northwest were magical for us and our young family.

On board was a large binder full of detailed instructions on how to manage the boat, along with a log book. It was mandatory that each skipper fill out the log in detail after each use. Where did we go? How long were we gone? It contained notes on damage and any repairs that were made, fuel consumption, sailing conditions, and supplies purchased for the good of the boat. The log also asked whether the boat was clean and stocked after the last use and, most importantly, had we checked "done" next to the 25 actions necessary to return the boat safely to the marina and in good order for the next user. And if not, why not? The management company that looked after the fleet checked each boat when it came in to be certain everything on the list was done properly.

The most important lesson we learned as a family during the ten years we shared this beautiful boat was a variation on "The Boy Scout Rule." Instead of leaving the campsite better than we found it, we left the boat better than we found it. All of the partners took pride in doing the hard work to return her in Bristol condition because we all truly cared about the next person's experience. Often we would leave a small gift for the children, or a bottle of wine, or a handwritten note about a great anchorage we found during our week that they might like to try. Each boat in the program was its own small community.

We learned the ropes on Butterscotch.

Eventually we bought a similar boat of our own that we christened *Butterscotch* in honor of Michael's father who had recently passed away. He was a fine gentleman who loved generous servings of both butter and scotch. We continued sailing for ten years, and spent many wonderful weeks living on the boat. We sold her just before we left on our Senior Nomads' adventure, and it was hard. But spending time living in a small space, keeping things tidy, and traveling with minimal personal belongings helped us appreciate how little we needed to be happy. That, along with sharing the *Pure Joy*, gave us many of the skills that make our current lifestyle work so well.

Fast forward to the summer of 2013. At first, Michael was concerned about our ages and our lack of experience as guests. But once we understood the importance reviews played in the community, we breathed a sigh of relief. If there was one thing we knew, it was how to leave a place as good, or better, than we found it. That meant we were in control of our own destiny within the Airbnb community. If we got good ratings from our hosts, we should have no trouble finding people willing to rent to us. So we strove to become the best guests we could be. I am happy to report we've had well over 100 great reviews, and only one where a host in Paris said they wouldn't have us back because we were "hard to satisfy." I'm actually quite proud of that one.

When we arrive at an Airbnb, we consider it our home for however long we stay so we treat it as if it were our own. We can't speak for anyone but ourselves, but for us that means we try to leave it just a little bit better than we found it. Maybe because we miss having a real home to look after, we start puttering. Michael is a great one for fixing little things like loose handles on pots or a wobbly toilet seat. We've bought new pads for the bottoms of chairs, replaced light bulbs, weeded the garden, fixed a squeaky door, unclogged the drains, left a casserole in the freezer, fed the cat, and placed flowers on the table.

No matter how long the stay, we believe all guests should treat their Airbnb as their own or, better yet, as if they were staying the weekend at their mother-in-law's. That would require them to pick up after themselves, wash their dishes, take out the garbage, strip the bed, wipe out the sink and tub, and sweep the floor. If they use, eat, or drink the last of something, replace it. And don't leave anything in the fridge that isn't fresh or a gift. Finally, leave a thank-you note, even if it's on a napkin.

We try to send a message to our hosts the day after we've settled in to let them know how happy we are with our choice and find something special to comment on, such as how comfortable the bed is, or the speed of the Internet, or how much we enjoyed the wine or other welcome gift. This starts our

Show your appreciation.

relationship off on a good note, and hopefully puts our hosts at ease. During our longer stays, we touch base with our hosts a few more times just to let them know everything is fine. If the roles were reversed, I know we would appreciate the occasional check-in.

Of course things can and sometimes do go wrong. If the hot water doesn't work or the WiFi is sputtering or an expectation based on the listing isn't met, we follow the US Department of Homeland Security rule: "If You See Something, Say Something." In our experience, hosts want us to be safe and comfortable and experience a "5-star" stay. That means they will usually do whatever it takes to solve a problem. It's only fair to give them that chance because they may be unaware of the situation. Failing to let the host know your concerns, or posting a negative review without having given them the chance to rectify the problem during your stay, means nobody wins.

The reverse is true, too. Guest reviews are equally important so we hope that if we're doing something that makes you uncomfortable or goes against your house rules, let us know.

When Michael and I leave your home, we hope we can say "thank you" and "goodbye" in person. It's also the best time to discuss anything that may need your attention, or suggestions we might have for improvement. If we don't get the chance to see you again, we'll send you a message telling you we've left so you can begin preparations for the next guest.

So what does being a great guest have to do with you becoming a great host? More than you might think because you can do several things that help and encourage us to become 5-star guests. First, if your house is clean, orderly, and organized, we are more likely to keep *and* leave it that way. You know the old adage "Garbage in, garbage out?" We do take the garbage out, so please tell us where it goes and leave enough garbage bags to do the job (sorry, that's a pet peeve). A few pods of laundry soap and dishwashing soap are also welcome. If you leave cleaning supplies, we may actually use them!

There can't be too much information.

If you have a house manual that describes how things work — the television, the washing machine, the dishwasher, stove top, oven, shower, hot water, heat or AC, and anything else that turns on or off — the less likely we will break or misuse them, or bother you with unnecessary questions. I've cooked in 110 kitchens and can assure you every oven has its quirks.

Washing machines might look the same, but when it comes time to commit your clothes to a three-hour European wash cycle, it's good to know how it works. I'm also glad to find the manufacturers' manuals for appliances on hand, too, because they're written in nearly every language with diagrams.

Here is one final, and maybe our most important, suggestion to help you create an exceptional experience for your guest – and for you as a host. Pack your suitcase and stay in your own Airbnb for a few nights. Pretend you're the guest, and don't bring anything you wouldn't pack for an enjoyable weekend away.

Be conscious of the guest experience from the moment you put the key in the lock. One thing hosts often forget to share is where the button is in the lobby to open the door when you are leaving the building. Be sure to enter and exit after dark as well so you can experience coming and going at night. Can you find the outside lock in the dark? If the lobby is dark, where is the light switch?

Next, unpack your suitcase. Is there room for your belongings in a closet and a few drawers, and is there a shelf in the bathroom for your toiletries? Now it's time to relax after a long day of "travel." Is the space inviting and the couch comfortable? Is the lighting warm and pleasant? Turn on the TV a few times with a fresh eye to see how the remotes work (pretend you don't know). Is there a stack of city maps, *current* tourist brochures, and a house manual to review while you

8

What We've Learned

About ourselves and the world

"A great marriage is not when the
'perfect couple' comes together.
It is when an imperfect couple learns
to enjoy their differences."

— Dave Meurer

Good companions in Paris.

During our three-year odyssey, Michael and I have learned a few things about ourselves and each other. That can happen when you are with a person twenty-four hours a day, seven days a week in small spaces. You'd think after thirty-eight happily married years there wouldn't be much you didn't know about your spouse. But for most of those years, we were working full time and raising a family. And of course, there were after-school and volunteer commitments as well. So at times we found ourselves bumping into each other in the kitchen on the way out the door, or just before we fell into bed. Who had time to really "go deep" into our relationship outside of the odd "reset" brought on by a disagreement. And even then, we went right back to our busy day-to-day lives.

Once our children were out of the house we had more time to enjoy each other's company, which we always had, and to begin thinking about what our future might hold. Still, we continued to be busy with work, community projects and our family – for a while, there was a steady stream of grandchildren arriving. Nonetheless, we felt the tide was shifting.

That brings us back to our discovery of Airbnb and the possibility of spending time traveling together. We called it our "Gap Year for Seniors." To our surprise and delight, it's become more than that – it has become a lifestyle that we absolutely love and fully embrace. And it's brought us closer together than ever. As Michael often tells people, "Don't try this unless you're traveling with your best friend." So true.

As you recall, Michael is creative but also a linear thinker. His idea of getting from A to B is different from mine. He's a straight-line kind of guy while I am always willing to see what's around the next corner. One of our biggest challenges is having a set plan for a given day and I add an additional day's worth of activities to the agenda, often because I just discovered something happening that we just shouldn't miss. On these occasions, his gentle insistence that we keep to our original plan usually works out for the best. But I still wonder if we missed something amazing!

But every so often he admits my way of thinking gets us through some situations where conventional wisdom doesn't apply. Like the infamous Moscow Metro system.

Two years into our journey, we were finally in Russia, a country that had long been on our wish list. We had our Moscow host's instructions on how to find our Airbnb and we'd gotten as far as the metro station. Now we were standing with our luggage at the top of a very old, very steep escalator that would take us nearly 25 stories below street level.

Since we were about to take our first ride on this notorious subway where there is very little English translation on signage or maps, we thought we should have some idea of the direction we were heading and where we should get off before committing to a 15-minute journey through the earth's core. My suggestion was this: "All we need to do is figure out how to form a simple English-sounding word from the Cyrillic letters for the end destination, like "Soko" from Sokolnicheskayae. Then we'll figure out which line that is and the platform it leaves from." Easy enough. Once we got on the train, Google Maps said to get off 7 stops later at "Mayo" for Mayakovskaya. We quickly learned you couldn't see the station destination signage from the train so we both nervously counted the stops on our fingers and hoped for the best. As we continued to travel around Moscow, we added even more words to our metro lexicon so that by the end of the week I'd say, "Let's catch Napkin to Toy Story" and we knew exactly what I meant. There was definitely some satisfaction in that.

That might have been the moment we crossed our personal Rubicon and realized we could do this anywhere. We were officially world travelers and, regardless of language or cultural norms, we could figure out how to navigate any city. We could find an Airbnb within our budget and make it our new home. And we could enjoy life and everything a new location had to teach us for as long as we chose to keep traveling.

Looking back, there were lots of other "aha" moments that gave us the confidence we could do this. Like eight months into our journey when we decided to rent our home in Seattle for a second year, which would mean we would be homeless for another 16 months. Or when we were home after a year and a half of travel for our son Chris' wedding and decided to go back on the road – only this time we bought one-way tickets because we didn't know when we'd return.

Of course, the most obvious decision that demonstrated our commitment to this new lifestyle came after two and a half years of living in other peoples' homes – the decision to sell our house in Seattle. People often ask if that was difficult, and amazingly enough it wasn't. It felt like the right thing to do at that time and we've never looked back. As Frank Sinatra said, "You only go around once in life, but if you play your cards right, once is enough." We were dealt a good hand and the house sold quickly.

We've been many places where bets were being laid on the

future of the country and we witnessed history being made. If we weren't pursuing this adventure we wouldn't have walked the streets of Sarajevo with our host who grew up under siege. We wouldn't have met the President of Kosovo at a pubic press conference in the park that led to lunch the next day with the director of the United Nations Development Program.

Current events come to life in Moscow.

We wouldn't have spent a week in Jerusalem during Passover, along with an entire day in Palestine where our personal guide explained their side of the conflict. While in Moscow, Michael wouldn't have stood with tears in his eyes next to the memorials left on the Bolshoy Moskvoretsky Bridge for Boris Nemtsov, a Russian physicist, statesman, and dissident who was assassinated in February 2015. We wouldn't have walked across the disputed border in Nicosia, Cyprus, or spent a day in Transnistria, the break-away republic between Moldova and Ukraine. Or seen Berlin as it is now. Or, for better or worse, been in Paris on November 13th, at the 2015 Airbnb Open, when terrorists attacked the city. Our three weeks in Cuba would still be on a wish list somewhere, and we wouldn't have been glued to the television in London watching the Brexit vote in the summer of 2016.

We've had the good fortune to look back on history as well. We stood quietly in both the American and German WWII Memorials in Normandy and visited the Jewish cemetery in Kraków. A day spent in Belfast gave us insight into "The Troubles" in Ireland. And from the top of mount Lycabettus in Athens we saw ancient Greece spread out before us, and in Turkey we touched the stones of Ephesus, a near-perfect city built in the 10th century B.C.

A history lesson in Belfast.

Throughout our travels, we've also learned we can live with so much less than we thought. Most of our needs are met by what we continuously curate and keep in our suitcases, and the few things we purchase along the way. We often leave items behind – like books and olive oil with our hosts when flying to our next destination, or when taking brief trips back to Seattle where we repack lighter each time. It's far more interesting to travel with space for a few great finds from a vintage store or open market than have your bag crammed to capacity with no room for new, even if temporary, additions to brighten a tired wardrobe or add a little sizzle to a meal.

What we've found that doesn't weigh an ounce but we couldn't live without is the Internet. We follow the headlines, stay in touch with family and friends, plan our travels, and keep endlessly entertained using a myriad of sources. This whole Senior Nomad adventure would not be possible without our Kindles, laptops, iPhones, and an iPad, along with the apps we use daily. We are far too old to be clutching a dog-eared copy of *The Rough Guide* and living out of backpacks so we are committed to staying current with technology, although Michael's daypack is so heavy with all our gear he occasionally needs to find a physical therapist to work on what we call "Sherpa Shoulder." And we can always Skype our son Christopher if we need technical help. Don't all parents do that?

Some people ask how we manage in countries where little

English is spoken. Unfortunately, neither Michael nor I speak a second language, but even if we did, we'd still have a communication barrier – so far we've navigated in forty different languages. So we've learned the universal language of courtesy. Whether online with our hosts or face-to-face with strangers, learning a few basic words of greeting along with "please," "thank you," and "I am so sorry!" in the local language will almost always get you a smile. You'd be amazed at the number of people you meet who actually *do* speak English – when they choose. Plus, Google Translate has saved our bacon (no matter what it's called in other countries) many times.

Some things translate in any language.

After traveling for this long, we are beginning to reflect on how it all began, and where it has taken us. We certainly couldn't have imagined being on the road for over three years!

At this point it may seem a bit extreme but, like any major change in life, you become used to it. It's now normal for us. Sort of like people who climb the world's highest peaks – oh, yawn, another day, another mountain.

How many devices can you use at once?

Thanks to Michael's many spreadsheets, we can review with accuracy whether the original hypothesis that captured our imagination holds true: *Would it be possible to reduce expenses on the road so low that we could use our social security and retirement savings to travel the world for the same amount of money we would spend if we were retired at home in Seattle?* As it turns out, the answer is: not quite.

We couldn't live a comfortable lifestyle, no matter how budget conscious we are, as Senior Nomads for the same amount of money prudent retirees spend. But the cost is not much more. In fact, the extra 15–20% we've spent each year has been money well spent. The experience we've gained is, as MasterCard would say, "Priceless." And who knows how long we have on this earth?

Before becoming The Senior Nomads, Michael and I both worked full time and made decent salaries. And while we did our monthly budgeting together, and were aware of most of our spending, each of us had leeway to spend money personally as we saw fit. That's all changed. Now we write down every single expense in a notebook, tape in the receipts, and then jot down everything we did that day. At the end of the month the daily tallies are added into the ominous Master Spending Spreadsheet. We've filled a dozen of these journals so they are something we will always treasure. But the scrutiny of daily

One of a dozen daily journals so far.

spending took some getting used to for me. You want a receipt for that Diet Coke? Really?

The process has become sort of fun, and it certainly helps us look at our journey in the rear-view mirror. And the accountability to each other reduces spending in a big way, with the added benefit that there are rarely arguments around money. It also brings us closer in our partnership as we make plans around where we are heading next – on this journey, or beyond.

Almost everyone, from strangers on the train to newspaper reporters (and of course our family), asks us how long we will keep up this nomadic life. Our answer is simple. As long as we are having fun, learning every day, staying close to budget, and still in love. So far, so good.

9

Our Good Fortune
Inspiring others to live their dream

"Twenty years from now you will be more disappointed by the things that you didn't do than by the ones you did do. So throw off the bowlines. Sail away from the safe harbor. Catch the trade winds in your sails. Explore. Dream. Discover."

– H. Jackson Brown, Jr.

One year into our travels, Michael and I thought Airbnb might be interested in knowing we were literally living our lives in Airbnb homes. We assumed our experience wasn't what the founders had in mind when they launched their home-sharing company, but maybe they'd be amused to discover two retired people who took it to such an extreme. We believed then, and still do today that, without the vision behind Airbnb to build a community where anyone could belong anywhere in the world and there are no strangers, we might have flamed out a long time ago.

We belong anywhere!

At that time we didn't know anyone at Airbnb. So Michael crafted an email with a short history of The Senior Nomads and sent it to a few departments such as marketing@airbnb, jobs@airbnb, and the general mailbox. Then we waited to see if, out of the thousands of emails they must receive every day, someone might notice ours. Two weeks later we heard from a person in the communications department who happened to be from Seattle. What followed was more than we ever imagined.

On February 25, 2015, six months after that initial contact, *The New York Times* featured us in a story that filled two full pages. That story became the number one emailed article for the next two days, and number five for another full week. We write a blog where I ramble about our adventures for ourselves and our family and friends. At the time the story broke, we had an average of around 100 followers. After the story ran, the blog received a mind-boggling 14,500 hits the first day, and over 50,000 hits the first week. It was like having George Clooney drop by unannounced and me answering the door, bleary eyed in my Hello Kitty pajamas and no make-up. I scrambled back through the blog to correct typos and scrub overly personal sharing. Probably too late. Our Senior Nomad email address linked to the blog also overflowed with hundreds of comments and questions from around the world. Here's the response from Steven Kurutz, the talented *New York Times* reporter who wrote the story when Michael asked him what he thought of the reaction:

"I'm glad you've noticed the great response on your blog and Face-book page. The reach of The Times is something to behold. Still, what happened with the Nomads story is very rare. To sit atop the most

emailed list for two days is a true feat. I can recall only one or two other stories I've done that received that level of sustained interest.

As I said, it's a testament to the appeal of what you and Debbie are doing. We all, young and old, wish we could downsize our lives and take a great journey. Also, the Times reader who emails stories to friends and relatives tends to be an older one (younger readers simply cut and paste links or tweet or text) and so the story was catnip to those who are nearing or living in retirement. I think that explains why it sat in the top spot for two days."

Michael took time to respond to each of the emails personally and found, to Steven's point, that the one message that came through loud and clear was that people were inspired by our story. Many of the comments and questions came from people either retired or close to retirement who received the article from their grown children. Obviously it was a nudge to get them to rethink their plans! That meant a lot to us because our own four offspring are supportive and proud of us. And while they miss us, in some ways we "chat" more often than we ever did since we can Skype and FaceTime from anywhere in the world.

In fact, our oldest son Alistair and his wife Jenny were so inspired they quit their dream jobs in Portland, sold their cars, stored their stuff, rented their house, and hit the road for a one-year lap around the world with our 8- and 10-year-old grandchildren. They called it the Campbell Amble and made their way through 24 countries and lived in 35 Airbnbs.

The world became a classroom, and it was a life-changing experience for them all. They are back in the states now and settling in Los Angeles where both parents found new jobs they love more than the ones they left in Portland. It just goes to show that following the dream of traveling the world can be done at any age, on any budget, and at any stage in life.

The Campbell Jr.s off to see the world!

Since *The New York Times* story appeared, we've had a steady stream of press coverage about our journey, including articles in *Condé Nast Traveler, The Huffington Post, The New York Post, AFAR* magazine and dozens of newspapers, radio interviews, and a TV appearance in Dublin. The questions are invariably the same. How did it all start? What inspired you to do this? How long will you continue? What advice do you have for living together twenty-four hours a day? Hopefully we've answered most of those questions in previous chapters.

Lunch with host Ariane and the local press in Aix.

The other commonly asked question is: Where was your favorite place? The answer to that one is a moving target. We couldn't make this journey without Airbnb as an endless source of places to live anywhere in the world — and we've been fortunate to stay in some great homes. The ones that do stand out, however, usually have more to do with the hosts and how they made our experience memorable by sharing their culture and their hospitality than the physical place or even the location.

Four years ago if a fortune teller had looked intensely at our palms and foretold, "You will stop work, rid yourself of your possessions, and travel the world spreading a message of inspiration to others. Oh, and you'll write a book," I'm sure we would have had a laugh, paid the fee, and said to each other, "Well... that was interesting" and not given it another thought. Today, I would go back to that brilliant fortune teller, offer a 5-star Trip

Advisor review, and triple whatever we had paid her because her prediction has more than come true!

Inspiring others to live their own dream, whatever that might be, is something that keeps us going and committed to sharing our story. We hope you've enjoyed reading about our experience of living life, and loving each other, one Airbnb at a time.

We count our blessings every day.

Appendix

Special thanks to our hosts who welcomed us into their homes and handed over their keys.

Alan • Alberto • Ale • Alejandro • Aleks • Alisa & Alius • Ana • Annie • Ante • Arbel • Ariane and Norbert • Blanca • Brice • Charlotte • Chiho Daniel • Dario • David • Dianne • Dominium Dubravka • Duscia • Edona • Elisabetta • Elodie Elza • Emir • Enrico • Enrique • Enzo • Eoin • Evelio & Silvia • Fabio • Farid • Fausto • Federica Frederico • Gaelle • Geoff • George • Gesine • Gilles Hana • Hande • Hanna • Hans • Helena • Irena Irene • Iria • Isabelle • Isil • Jelena • Johan • Jonas Juan • Juan Carlo • Julie • Karim • Katarina • Kate Kenneth • Kepa • Kiwi • Kristina • Laura • Lili Louise • Luis • Luke • Mariana • Markus • Marlys Mary • Michael • Milos • Monique • Narcis • Nina Olga • Oliwia • Pamela & Ted • Paolo • Paul • Petra Pietro • Richard • Riitta • Rob • Roberto & Marta Robin • Ruben • Rutger • Ruth • Ryan • Samim Sanne • Scott • Serena • Sigrid • Silvio y Julia Sonia • Sophie • Stefanakis • Susan • Svetlana Tamara • Tilman • Tine • Tom • Vana • Vladimir Wendy • Yann • Yishai • Yonko

Homes on the Road

To view an Airbnb from this list type **www.airbnb.com/rooms/number** in your browser. For example, if you want to see the Airbnb in Aix-en-Provence enter **www.airbnb.com/rooms/507037**. Each city has the listing number on the far right unless it is no longer available. Those listings show Listing N/A.

CITY	COUNTRY	HOST	DATES		LISTING
Aix-en-Provence	France	Ariane	Mar	2016	507037
Amsterdam	Netherlands	Rutger	Aug	2013	1029865
Amsterdam	Netherlands	Wendy	Apr2015		1357751
Amsterdam	Netherlands	Johan	Jul	2016	664904
Andorra la Vella	Andorra	Monique	Apr	2016	7742165
Antwerp	Belgium	Isabelle	Jul	2015	4733497
Athens	Greece	Helena	Nov	2013	951594
Bainbridgel Isl, WA	USA	Robin	Aug	2014	678513
Baku	Azerbaijan	Farid	Aug	2016	5975657
Barcelona	Spain	Alejandro	Mar	2014	980152
Bari	Italy	Enzo	Feb	2015	1291786
Belgrade	Serbia	Duscia	Jun	2015	5517743
Bend, OR	USA	Ryan	Dec	2015	7869248
Berlin	Germany	Gesine	Oct	2013	Listing N/A
Bilbao	Spain	Juan	Nov	2014	3860584
Brno	Czech Republic	Daniel	May	2015	1712691
Brusssels	Belgium	Iria	Jul	2015	Listing N/A
Bucharest	Romania	Ana	Jul	2015	4202554
Budapest	Hungary	Kristina	Jun	2015	1126755
Budva	Montenegro	Milos	Jun	2016	1308391
Caen	France	Yann	Sep	2015	3153231
Cardenas	Cuba	Susan	Feb	2016	6019656
Chisinau	Moldova	Tamara	Aug	2015	1514277
Cienfuegos	Cuba	Enrico	Feb	2016	5877529
Cinque Terre	Italy	Pietro	May	2015	1136445
Cologne	Germany	Tilman	Jul	2015	6548097
Copenhagen	Denmark	Charlotte	Sep	2013	1348732
Dania Beach, FL	USA	Pamela	Jan	2016	9129877
Denver, CO	USA	Dianne	Mar	2016	5445148
Dinan	France	Kate	Aug	2015	2091218
Dublin	Ireland	Alan	Jun	2014	2809448
Dublin	Ireland	Roberto	Jun	2016	11647025
Dublin	Ireland	Luke	Jun	2016	10484866
Dubrovnik	Croatia	Dominium	Apr	2014	1065106

CITY	COUNTRY	HOST	DATES		LISTING
Edinburgh	Scotland	Dario	Jun	2014	1916313
Essaouria	Morocco	Frederico	Jan	2015	322238
Florence	Italy	Serena	Oct	2013	1368020
Galway	Ireland	Irene	Jun	2016	3723474
Girona	Spain	Narcis	Apr	2016	6229018
Gozo	Malta	Mary	Feb	2015	718401
Granada	Spain	Blanca	Dec	2014	1754593
Haarlam	Netherlands	Sanne	Apr	2015	5306203
Havana	Cuba	Julia	Feb	2016	5704246
Havana	Cuba	Evelio	Feb	2016	6103520
Helskinki	Finland	Riitta	Jul	2014	2302108
Hvar	Croatia	Ante	Apr	2014	607986
Hvar	Croatia	Katarina	May	2016	1089827
Istanbul	Turkey	Isil	Apr	2014	85717
Izmir	Turkey	Hande	Mar	2015	1626650
Jerusalem	Israel	Yishai	Apr	2015	1423284
Kiev	Ukraine	Olga	Aug	2016	1438181
Krakow	Poland	Oliwia	Jul	2016	351091
Larnaca	Cyprus	George	Mar	2015	1742220
Lecce	Italy	Fausto	Feb	2015	1374534
Lisbon	Portugal	Chiho	Nov	2013	495237
Ljubljana	Slovenia	Irena	May	2014	210296
London	UK	Richard	Feb	2014	1701111
London	UK	Rob	Jun	2016	12844785
Luxembourg City	Luxembourg	Lili	Dec	2014	Listing N/A
Lviv	Ukraine	Michael	Aug	2016	12864863
Madrid	Spain	Enrique	Nov	2014	991697
Marrakech	Morocco	Gilles	Jan	2015	1118641
Marrakech	Morocco	Karim	Jan	2015	219785
Mexico City	Mexico	Alberto	Jan	2016	5955186
Mexico City	Mexico	Juan Carlo	Jan	2016	1022380
Milan	Italy	Ale	Oct	2013	1137458
Minsk	Belarus	Olga	Aug	2016	2895472
Montpellier	France	Geoff	Mar	2014	677804
Moscow	Russia	Svetlana	Aug	2015	5747355
Naples	Italy	Elisabetta	Jan	2015	4469870
Nice	France	Scott	Feb	2014	Listing N/A
Nicosia	Cyprus	Paolo	Mar	2015	1829849
Oslo	Norway	Tine	Jun	2014	Listing N/A
Paris	France	Sophie	Dec	2013	204229
Paris	France	Jonas	May	2014	2471473
Paris	France	Julie	Jan	2015	1298997

CITY	COUNTRY	HOST	DATES		LISTING
Paris	France	Brice	Aug	2015	393975
Paris	France	Gaelle	Nov	2015	608289
Paris	France	Nina	Nov	2015	3991028
Paris	France	Gaelle	Mar	2016	608289
Paris	France	Elodie	Oct	2016	11803765
Parma	Italy	Laura	May	2015	1014113
Pezenas	France	Louise	Apr	2016	3637437
Podgorica	Montenegro	Dubravka	Jun	2015	188858
Portland, OR	USA	Scott	Sep	2015	5294566
Porto	Portugal	Luis	Sep	2015	6040148
Prague	Czech Republic	Hana	May	2015	5718458
Pristina	Kosovo	Edona	Jun	2015	1125537
Rhodes	Greece	Stefanakis	Mar	2015	1037492
Riga	Latvia	Tom	Jul	2014	124679
Rome	Italy	Federica	Mar	2014	406693
Salzburg	Austria	Markus	May	2015	Listing N/A
San Francisco, CA	USA	Kepa	Oct	2015	33578
San Miguel	Mexico	Mariana	Jan	2016	6569224
Santa Fe, NM	USA	Marlys	Mar	2016	7063159
Sarajevo	Bosnia	Emir	Apr	2014	420924
Seattle, WA	USA	Samim	Sep	2014	3238295
Senglea	Malta	Paul	Apr	2015	5139924
Seville	Spain	Daniel	Dec	2014	3857892
Skopje	Macedonia	Aleks	Jul	2015	717852
Sofia	Bulgaria	Yonko	Jul	2015	4543540
Split	Croatia	Vana	Apr	2014	1015070
Split	Croatia	Jelena	Apr	2016	11289569
St. Julian's	Malta	Fabio	Nov	2015	7400166
St. Petersburg	Russia	Vladimir	Aug	2015	4851244
Stockholm	Sweden	Hanna	Sep	2013	1434684
Tallinn	Estonia	Sigrid	Jul	2014	916482
Tas-Sliema	Malta	Kenneth	Mar	2015	1596489
Tel Avi	Israel	Arbel	Apr	2015	2935050
The Hague	Netherlands	Sonia	Jul	2016	3351313
Tiblisi	Georgia	Hans	Aug	2016	7594839
Trinidad	Cuba	Kiwi	Feb	2016	8141043
Victoria, BC	Canada	Annie	Aug	2014	844027
Vienna	Austria	Petra	May	2014	2023633
Vilnius	Lithuania	Alisa	Jul	2014	620586
Wexford	Ireland	Eoin	Jun	2014	1545588
Yerevan	Armenia	Ruben	Sep	2016	1371528
Zadar	Croatia	Elza	May	2016	3268300

Made in the USA
San Bernardino, CA
19 January 2020